I
AM
WORTH
IT

I AM WORTH IT

Jan D. Kelly
Barbara J. Winship

Nelson-Hall [nh] Chicago

Library of Congress Cataloging in Publication Data

Kelly, Jan D
  I am worth it.

  Includes index.
  1. Assertiveness (Psychology) 2. Interpersonal relations. 3. Defense mechanisms (Psychology)
I. Winship, Barbara J., joint author. II. Title.
BF575.A85K44   158'.1   78-26111
ISBN 0-88229-291-9

Copyright © 1979 by Jan D. Kelly and Barbara J. Winship

All rights reserved. No part of this book may be reproduced in any form without permission in writing from the publisher, except by a reviewer who wishes to quote brief passage in connection with a review written for broadcast or for inclusion in a magazine or newspaper. For information address Nelson-Hall Inc., Publishers, 111 North Canal Street, Chicago, Ill. 60606.

Manufactured in the United States of America

10   9   8   7   6   5   4   3   2   1

Contents

Introduction   vii

PART 1: YOUR RIGHTS   1

1. Childhood Lessons in Nonassertiveness   5
2. What Are Your Rights?   15

PART 2: THREE STYLES OF BEHAVING   27

3. A Case Study in Nonassertiveness   31
4. Nonassertiveness   39
5. Aggressiveness   48
6. Assertiveness   58

PART 3: A VERBAL RESPONSE MODEL OF ASSERTIVENESS   67

7. Empathy   71
8. Conflict   77
9. Action   83
10. A Case Study in Assertiveness   90
11. Nonverbal Components of Assertiveness   99
12. Negotiation   104
13. Self-Diagnosis   114
14. Assertiveness: An Avenue to Intimacy   118

Index   123

Introduction

This book is intended for any person who wishes to change his way of interacting with other people. It offers a specific, workable model of assertiveness that an individual can apply in any interpersonal relationship or interchange. The completely assertive person is nonexistent; at one time or another each of us has responded nonassertively to a spouse, a boss, a relative, a friend, a child, or an acquaintance. The following questions point up ways that people typically respond in many areas of their lives. Ask yourself these questions and ask to whom you respond in the way described:

    1. Do you let others inconvenience you (make you wait, demand that you do something)?

    2. Do you hesitate to make requests of others (ask for a raise, ask to change an appointment time)?

3. Do you accept situations you don't like rather than assume responsibility for changing them?

4. Do you let others decide what you are going to do (accept what others say without question, put other people's needs and wants before your own)?

5. Do you continually get others to take care of you (persuade your spouse or a friend to make phone calls or run errands for you)?

6. Do you retreat into yourself when problems arise (withdraw when hassled, become depressed, sulk, "calm your nerves" by taking pills)?

7. Do you remain agreeable and deny getting upset when things make you angry?

8. Do you let your spouse, friends, or relatives impose on you or take advantage of you (do whatever your spouse asks, let relatives visit longer than you desire)?

9. Do you leave grievances uncorrected (fail to return damaged merchandise, correct false statements made about you)?

10. Do you often get headaches or backaches when you feel angry or helpless?

Undoubtedly you saw yourself in one or more of the examples, or the examples caused you to think of similar situations that you have encountered. Everyone does these things sometimes. However, if you frequently find yourself feeling at the mercy of the actions of others or are unable to act as you would like, you can learn to feel and act differently—to refuse friends and neighbors who impose on you; to ask for favors, help, or raises; to set the record straight when wronged—and alleviate the fear that others will reject you for it.

Part 1

Your Rights

How often have you behaved in ways that are nonassertive to avoid being called selfish, cold, incompetent, uncaring, or stupid?

For fear of being rejected or labeled as "pushy," most people often react in ways that are contrary to their desires and beliefs. Most nonassertive people consider rejection to be the most threatening possible consequence of any action. And it is out of this basic fear of rejection that much of the complicated, self-defeating behavior of nonassertive individuals occurs. Rather than admit the fear of rejection, most nonassertive people dupe themselves into believing that if they comply with others' demands they eventually will be rewarded. By denying oneself or by delaying one's personal gratification until later, the person perpetuates the myth that "something better" will happen in the future. In essence, he says, "I won't make waves now, but I'll get what I want from them later."

For example, a neighbor calls and asks you to keep her children while she and her husband go away for the weekend. You have a busy weekend coming up, and you don't want to have her children at your house. You are afraid to refuse, however, because you believe that she will think you are selfish; you believe she won't like you anymore or will be angry. Instead of admitting this fear of rejection, you grudgingly agree to keep the children, *telling yourself* that the reason is your hope that she will volunteer to care for *your* kids when *you* go on vacation.

Here is another example of how the nonassertive person engages in self-denial or delaying gratification in order to avoid confrontation and fear of catastrophic expectation. A co-worker talks constantly during working hours. You are afraid to tell her to stop because you think she will get angry, and you are afraid to tell your boss because you don't want to be a "snitch." Instead of confronting her, you tell yourself that sooner or later the boss will notice and take appropriate action or that one of you will be transferred to another office. You tell yourself that you will retain your reputation as a pleasant, uncomplaining worker.

Finally, your dry cleaner lost one of the shirts you sent for cleaning, but you didn't notice it until you got home. You are afraid to go back because you think the attendent will be angry and accuse you of leaving the missing shirt at home. You tell yourself that if you don't complain, you won't jeopardize your good relationship with the cleaners, and you will get good service in the future.

These examples identify some of the reasons individuals use to keep from being assertive. Part 1 will deal with an individual's rights in a variety of situations and the reasons why people believe they have no rights.

All of the expectations concerning rejection, reward, or punishment are learned. A baby is not born fearing that he or she will be rejected or believing that if he gives in now, he will be rewarded later. He knows only what he wants and needs. He is born open and receptive to the world in which he lives.

1
Some Childhood Lessons in Nonassertiveness

It is our contention that a baby's earliest attempts at communication are clear and direct statements. For example, a baby cries in one tone when he is hungry and cries in another when hurt, wet, and so on. Thus it would appear that he comes into the world asserting himself in as direct a manner of communication as he knows. He protests loudly when his needs aren't met. It is obvious that the child knows he needs food, sleep, and care.

Into the baby's perfect need system enter two adults—his parents—with their own needs. Their world is composed not only of survival needs but of needs for approval and fears of rejection, involving the child, and others. Their previous training has led them to believe that children do not have rights and that it is their duty to respond to the environment rather than to the child-parent relationship.

Therefore, the relationship that develops between the parents and their child is one of integrating him into a system that basically teaches that his needs are subject to the control of others. Thus a power struggle begins between the parents and the child.

For example, when an infant is hungry, he cries to be fed. The parents hear his cry, but, desiring approval from the doctor, whose instructions are to feed the child every four hours, the mother attempts to ignore the crying. The struggle is resolved in one of two ways. First, the child may be fed when the mother tires of the crying and, with feelings of anger or resentment, gives in. Often she will rationalize by saying to herself, "This time I'll feed him off schedule, but never again." Second, the struggle may be resolved by the child's complying and waiting until the end of the four-hour period.

Later in childhood, while visiting an aunt, the child comes in the house and requests a drink of water. He is hot and thirsty from playing in the summer sun. The aunt replies, "You can't be thirsty; you just had a glass of milk for lunch an hour ago." The child is confused because he is thirsty and because the aunt didn't fill his request. Instead of trusting the child to know his wants and needs, the aunt indirectly answered the child by attempting to read his mind. The result of this type of interaction leaves the child confused about who to trust to know what's best.

He also begins to learn to communicate indirectly; that is, to not answer direct questions with direct answers. If the aunt were busy or wanted the child to help himself, it would have been better to say so rather than be indirect.

From these early attempts at asserting himself, the child begins to learn that he has to forego his immediate personal needs and comply with the demands of others—his parents or other authority figures. He learns that he must allow others' needs to precede his own if he is to survive. He risks being punished or rejected if he continues to demand that his needs be met immediately and on his own terms.

As he grows older he is told repeatedly that if he expresses his needs he is being selfish; and he is made to feel guilty. This message, when repeated over and over, ultimately forces him to modify his initial natural response to himself. He is no longer sure of what he wants. He learns that directness and honesty about his personal needs are ineffective, because his parents teach him to be dishonest about himself. They tell him he doesn't have the right to think, feel, or act without their permission. Furthermore, he is taught not to express feelings or opinions—especially if they are negative or in conflict with others' ideas. A son angered by his father's refusal to spend time with him is told by his mother, "Don't say you hate your father. After all, he works hard to give you all the things you want!" Or, "You don't really hate your sister. What if she died? Then think how sorry you'd be." If he expresses his anger—or even feels it—he is taught that he ought to feel bad. Eventually he comes to believe that his anger is wrong and that he must not admit to it.

From these experiences the child is taught not to express his true feelings. He is taught that he should like everybody regardless of what they do to him. Another lesson that the child learns during his development is that he must not truly express his feelings about his successes and failures. If he is excited about his success he is told not to be a braggart; if he shares his feelings of hurt or pain he is told not to feel sorry for himself. Again, he is taught that it isn't his right to express genuine feelings. He is told that he must leave their expression to others. He may say, "I don't think I'm going to do very well on this test." His father responds, "Don't be silly; you're smart." If a child says, "I got an *A*," his parents may respond, "We've never expected anything less," thus deflating the child's pride in his accomplishment.

Another lesson kids learn is that they don't have the right to schedule their own time. A mother may spend hours selecting a dress for herself, but she allows her child only a few minutes to choose a toy. Another example is the timing of household chores. When a mother says, "Feed the dog," she means *right now,* not when the child finishes the game he is playing. On the other hand, when the child asks for a drink of water he is often told, "Wait until I finish what I'm doing." From such examples children learn that they don't have rights to make decisions about when to do something, but their parents do.

A child is taught to respect his elders, whether they deserve it or not. He must respect them for their age, rank, or family relationship. He must endure grandmother's hugs even when he doesn't want to be hugged. He must tolerate boredom, disgust, and anger in silence or risk punishment.

Kids learn to speak only when spoken to. An updated version of this is: "Don't ask questions. Don't be curious. Don't bother me." But when the child acts without complete and thorough knowledge and then fails, he is reprimanded with the question, "Why didn't you ask me?" A daughter is told, without any instructions, to do the laundry and uses too much soap. Her mother yells, "Why didn't you ask me how much to use?" The message is: Do as you're told even though you don't have sufficient information. A father tells his son to get him a wrench but fails to say which type or size he wants. After attempting four times to get the right one, the son feels stumped and discouraged. In both cases the child feels that *he* is the one at fault.

Children are taught that they are not capable of making choices and are provided with little, if any, opportunity to learn how to choose. This lesson comes from the parents' concern that the child be a reflection of them rather than an independent individual. Children aren't allowed to decide what clothes to wear or what clothes go together. Mothers dictate such choices not because they are important to the child, but because the mother would be embarrassed if someone thought her child was carelessly or inappropriately dressed. Unmatched socks, for example, would imply that she was not a good mother.

Another thing children learn is that they can't solve their own problems and are therefore dependent on others to come up with solutions for them. Because they aren't allowed to make decisions, they never learn to take responsibility for what they do. For example, fights between siblings are often settled by the parents, who thus deprive their children of the opportunity to learn the natural consequences of their actions. The child may learn to run to his mother after a fight, counting on her to take the necessary action to resolve the disagreement.

From lessons like these, a child learns to give up his rights. As he matures he learns the subtleties of being an adult. He is told to tell the truth but at the same time taught to be dishonest. He watches his parents entertain guests graciously and then later hears them discuss their dislike of the people who were invited. Or, when a neighbor comes to borrow a cup of sugar, he hears his mother say, "Any time. I'm glad to loan you anything you need." After the neighbor leaves, the mother says to her son, "Doesn't she know it's rude to borrow?" When the son asks why she loaned the sugar, his mother says, "You have to be nice to people." She thus teaches the child deception.

Adolescents learn a series of subtle messages that begin with the word *don't*. "Don't be too smart" is one. It translates into "Don't get too good grades because others won't like you," or "If you're too smart you won't get a husband." This rule is further translated into "Be humble." If you're outstanding you'll be different—an outcast —and thus be left alone and alienated.

People learn not to say what they think, because (1) they might be right and nobody likes a smart aleck, or (2) more often they might be wrong. To be right or wrong invites embarrassment or rejection, since you will be singled out. People learn not to let others know how they feel because it shows weakness and makes others uncomfortable. Weakness makes one vulnerable to attack. And showing emotions puts the other person in an awkward position because he doesn't know how to relate or react to an expression of feelings.

As a consequence of all these years of conditioning, some individuals become afraid to act independently. They reach adulthood feeling confused about who they are and depend on others to validate their existence. This position of nonassertiveness appears to be their only choice, since they have learned so well the fear of rejection by others. Nonassertive people conform to external control in order to reduce their anxiety and not feel guilty. They can be sure of the outcome of their actions if they behave in this manner, for being nonassertive results in predictable behavior from others and reduces fear of the unknown.

Even though such a pattern of behavior evokes predictable responses, it leaves the nonassertive person unable to communicate effectively with a spouse, merchants, supervisors, friends, and children. A wife may feel that she doesn't want to entertain her mother-in-law, but she is unable to tell that to her husband for fear he will be angry and reject her. A man is unwilling to return a sweater to a store even though it doesn't fit because he fears an embarrassing scene. An employee is unwilling to request a change in the vacation schedule because he doesn't want to impose on anyone else. A couple tolerate a neighbor's dog that barks at night because they fear that their relationship with the neighbor will become strained and uncomfortable if they complain. Finally, a father is unable to say no to his adolescent son who needs to be driven across town at the last minute, because he fears his son's anger and rejection.

12   Your Rights

Read the following situations and write on the space provided what a child or teenager learns from the interaction. Then write several examples from your own experience that identify what you learned about nonassertiveness while growing up.

1. Billy's class has returned from a visit to the office of a local politician who gave them a lecture on how the city government works. When the teacher asks for comments, Billy says, "I thought that was boring; he talked as if we didn't know anything." The teacher replies, "Mr. Cates is a very experienced office holder; I'm sure he gave us all a valuable lesson in local government."
Billy learns to say only what others want to hear; his opinions are invalid. _____
_____
_____

2. Angela is absorbed in her favorite afternoon cartoons on TV when her mother calls from the kitchen to demand that she stop what she is doing and immediately come to set the table. Angela answers, "I'll be there just as soon as this cartoon is over." Her mother replies, "I said right now. All you ever do is sit in front of that TV set."
Angela learns _____
_____
_____

3. Morgan is busily engaged in his homework when his father passes by his room on his way to the kitchen. Morgan asks, "Would you please bring

Some Childhood Lessons in Nonassertiveness 13

me a glass of coke on your way back?" His father replies, "Get your own; I'm not your servant." Morgan thinks to himself, earlier this evening when Dad was reading the paper and I walked by, he asked me to bring him a cup of coffee since I was on my way to the kitchen.
Morgan learns _____
_____
_____

4. While walking back to their car after doing the weekly marketing with his mother, Fritz overhears his mother mumble to herself that she was shortchanged one dollar by the cashier. He asks her, "Why don't you go back and ask for your money?" She tells him, "What's the use. It's only a dollar anyway."
Fritz learns _____
_____
_____

5. Your situation _____
_____
_____

You learned _____
_____
_____

6. Your situation _____
_____
_____
_____

14 Your Rights

You learned _____
_____
_____
_____

The purpose of this chapter has been to familiarize you with some of the ways that people are taught over a lifetime to be nonassertive. Special attention was paid to the early lessons about being nonassertive that children and teenagers experience. Some of the ways that you were taught to be nonassertive are in your awareness now.

2

What Are Your Rights?

All the examples in Chapter 1 show ways in which people learn not to assert their personal rights. Naturally, children taught such lessons are likely to fail to assert their rights as adults. In order to establish a foundation for alternative responses in situations where one's rights are at stake, one must be aware that there are three individual rights that every person can claim for himself. They are (1) the right to rectify a wrong, (2) the right to refuse, and (3) the right to request. These three rights serve as the basis for a new set of attitudes toward living and interacting.

The Right to Rectify a Wrong

Every person has the right to correct injustices against himself. If his rights have been encroached upon he has the right as well as the responsibility to himself to rectify the injury that has been done.

On first thought you may believe that no wrongs have been done to you, but what about the time your supervisor accused you of being late for work when you were on time? What about the time you bought a defective shirt on sale but left it hanging unworn in your closet as a silent reminder of your nonassertiveness? Finally, what about the time your insurance agent told you he would pay the first quarterly premium on your policy but later when he sent you the bill you paid for it?

In these and numerous other examples you did not exercise the right to rectify a wrong. Instead, you expended emotional energy over a long period of time as you said nothing to your supervisor but stayed angry and felt abused, as you let the shirt hang in the closet but ruminated over your stupidity at not seeing the defect, and as you paid the insurance premium, angry at yourself for allowing this to happen.

An assertive person in each situation would have exercised his right of rectification. He would have directly stated to his supervisor that he had been on time. He would have returned the shirt to the store even though it was on sale. Finally, he would have refused to pay the insurance premium, since a previous agreement had been made.

The amount of energy, time, and money it takes *not* to rectify a wrong can be considerable, as illustrated in the following examples.

Several years ago one of the authors purchased a pair of shoes he did not really want. He did want—desperately—a pair of wing-tip Florsheim Imperials—the most "in" style as he was finishing his graduate work.

He saved the money he needed and went to purchase his shoes. The salesman replied that he did have a pair of wing-tip Florsheim Imperials, but they were the wrong size and color. He patiently encouraged the author to try them on and was able to convince him that they would be just fine! Of course, after one wearing it was obvious that they were not just fine, yet the author felt foolish returning them and really did not want the salesman to know he had been manipulated into buying them. In reality, however, he had allowed the salesman to take advantage of him and felt foolish every time he saw the shoes in the back of his closet. Three years and three wearings later they were discarded.

It would have been valid to assume that the store owner wanted to please his customers and that he would have exchanged the shoes or refunded the money, but the author had failed to exercise his right to rectify a wrong—to return the shoes.

The same is true when you order dinner in a restaurant. You have a right to assume that the owners want to please you and to serve you what you order. If you order a medium steak but are served a rare one, it is your right to correct the situation. However, many people accept the rare steak and either leave a penny tip or grumble on the way out that they will not return.

Another example of neglecting to rectify a wrong is that of a college professor and his wife who had saved their money for a nice house near the campus where he taught. They wanted students to feel free to visit and had envisioned their home as a haven for themselves as well as for the students. Instead, a neighbor began to monopolize their time, appearing every day for several hours. One day the wife confronted her husband, saying that he would have to talk to this neighbor who was driving her insane. The husband could not bring himself to do it. The tension grew, and before long the wife issued an ultimatum. If he didn't tell the neighbor to leave them alone, she would either leave him or they would have to sell the house! They sold the house at a tremendous loss, because neither of them was able to tell the neighbor that she was intruding on their privacy.

THE RIGHT TO REFUSE

Every person has the right to say no if he so desires. The right to refuse is an important cornerstone in building autonomy and independence in your life. Implicit in this right is your obligation to set limits acceptable to your beliefs and values. You may believe that it is unrealistic to refuse reasonable requests. But in your attempts to set your own limits, you will sometimes find it appropriate to refuse requests, even those that are important to the other person. For example, you have the right to refuse to buy light bulbs over the telephone from a handicapped person; you have the right to say no to your boss who wants you to drive across town to buy a jar of cold cream for his wife during your lunch hour. You have the right to say no to your teenage son who asks you late Sunday night to wash his gym clothes so he can take them to school Monday morning.

True, you *could* comply with each request. You *could* agree to buy light bulbs because they are for a worthy cause. You *could* justify going across town to buy the cold cream for your boss's wife because he is so busy. And you *could* launder your son's gym clothes so that he won't be penalized in class. However, each of these requests could have violated your rights and the limits that you set for yourself. You didn't need the light bulbs; you had already made plans for lunch; and you had planned to go to bed early on Sunday. By agreeing to each request you violated your right to refuse.

By being aware of choices you are able to set limits, and, once these limits have been established, you can define your rights. As easy as it may sound, refusing a request may be difficult, as illustrated in the following example. One of the authors once hired a man to cut her lawn. She did not know him, but he was recommended by a neighbor. When she came out to pay him, he was busy putting her new two-hundred-dollar lawn mower in the trunk of his car. He explained that he just wanted to borrow it and would return it the next week when he returned to cut the lawn again. The author felt trapped for some inexplicable reason—caught between the panic of his stealing her lawn mower and the horror of his thinking her untrusting if she did not allow him to take it. So she began to make excuses—"Well, I had planned to use it again tomorrow." That was not true, but her hope was that then he would not want to take it and she would not have to tell him no. Instead, he accepted her condition and said he would return the next morning. The author felt sick as she watched him drive away with her lawn mower and, needless to say, spent a restless night worrying that she'd never see it again. She was furious at herself for lacking the courage to say no and allowing him to take it.

Fears of rejection and/or confrontation can make it difficult to refuse no matter how unreasonable the request may be. The need to be regarded as a "good person" may cause an individual to give in to demands and be left feeling "stepped on," put upon, or controlled rather than in control of his life.

The Right to Request

Each person has the right to request—to ask for anything he wants if he so desires. Implicit in the right to request is your opportunity to set your own goals independent of outside pressures. Your requests reflect the goals you have set for yourself. You may believe that it is unwise to ask for something for fear of future retaliation or for fear that you will be imposed upon in return. However, if your requests are contingent on what might happen sometime in the future, your options are severely limited. You have the right to establish your own goals, even though there may be times when your requests, in line with your goals, may seem inappropriate to others.

For example, you have the right to request that a friend drive you to the airport to catch an early Sunday morning flight. You can also request a cutting of a favorite camellia from your neighbor's bush. Or you have the right to ask your employer to tell his wife that she should not bring her personal work to the office for you to type.

This right to request makes it possible for you to ask for simple things that will make life easier. You do not have to wait until you are in critical straits to request assistance, nor do you have to manipulate other people into offering their time, service, or money by dropping hints.

You can do without the cutting of the camellia bush, find your own way to the airport, and continue to feel resentful and pressured when the boss's wife brings you more letters to type, but you don't have to! You should not look at such requests as taking advantage but rather as asking for what you desire.

Requests for promotions, salary increases, vacation time, new clothes, afternoons off, and so on, all involve your desire to obtain from someone else something that will benefit you. You may not actually expect your favorite department store to stay open on Sunday so you can shop, but what harm is there in asking? If enough requests are made, the store may agree to open on Sundays. If you never request time off to take a special vacation, you will never know whether your request might have been granted. Your supervisor is not responsible for planning your life!

A central reason for not making requests of others is the expectation that something catastrophic might happen to you. This fear is based on the idea that the worst possible consequence will result from any action. In reality this is hardly ever the case. For example, you may fail to ask for Friday afternoon off for fear that your boss will fire you for making such an unreasonable request. In reality your boss will say yes or no, but probably would not even consider firing you.

Implicit in your three personal rights is the basis for an open and direct mode of communication. Imagine being in a relationship with another person in which each of you interacted on the basis of these rights—a relationship in which you granted the other person the same rights you granted yourself, and vice versa. You would know that you could request anything of him and he of you but that each of you would also reserve the right to refuse any request. A clear line of communication would be opened between you.

As fantastic and simple as this direct form of communication sounds, it is absent from most relationships. In its place are indirect dodges that circumvent clear interaction. By hinting or baiting or avoiding the other person you make him guess what you are thinking or asking and force him to read your mind. For example, your husband calls and asks if you would like to go to a movie when you both get off work. You really want to go to a play, but you say you're not sure you want to see the movie, hoping that he will *guess* that you would rather see the play.

This inability to make a clear statement of your feelings creates a confusing situation in which both you and he are assuming responsibility for each other while ignoring your own rights. The cost of this pattern of communication is loss of time, loss of directness, confusion, and possibly anger at each other—he is angry because you rejected his idea; you are angry because he didn't know what you wanted. The communication pattern between you is common and involves an intricate process of learning.

Because of this learned pattern, it is easy to continue giving up personal rights. It is simpler to stay within the system, since there is less hassle, less fear of rejection, and greater safety. One is able to rely on old patterns of behavior and is not made to feel guilty for "rocking the boat."

A man who never stands up for himself lives in fear of being rejected by others because each person has different expectations of him. If he pleases one, he risks rejection from another. To please his wife, for example, he is likely to displease his mother. He constantly balances feelings and actions imposed by others. He expends a tremendous amount of emotional energy and time maintaining his relationship with each person as he carefully seeks permission from each to exist. If he never lets anyone know who he is and what he wants, he leaves them to decide from their own points of view. He lives behind masks placed on him by others and changes faces to agree with his current surroundings. Like a chameleon, a person who gives up his rights and changes color with the surrounding schema never shows his own true colors, his own worth. Thus, he never risks being vulnerable, but the quality of his life may be poorer than that of the person who risks self-exposure by making requests or refusals or rectifying wrongs.

Write examples of situations in which you have failed to assert your basic rights.

1. You failed to refuse (an unwanted date, an errand, an uninvited guest, a committee appointment):

   _____
   _____
   _____

2. You failed to make a request (a well-deserved promotion, a favor, someone's attention or time):

   _____
   _____
   _____

3. You failed to rectify a wrong (an accusation that you lied; an implication that you don't do your share of the work; an imposition on your time):

   _____
   _____
   _____

Think about times when you have asserted your rights even though you were afraid of the other person's reaction. What did the other person really do:

1. When you refused a request? _____
   _____
   _____

2. When you made a request? _____
   _____
   _____

3. When you rectified a wrong? _____
   _____
   _____
   _____

Part 2

Three Styles of Behaving

Now that we have identified the basic rights that we believe all people possess and discussed the necessary attitudes for accepting and acting on those rights, we will devote this part of the book to a description of behaviors and attitudes typical of everyday life and a description of the more desirable assertive behavior. This part is divided into four chapters. The first chapter is a case study of a husband and wife whose behaviors vary from nonassertive to aggressive, depending on the situation with which they are confronted. Following this case study are two chapters that describe, respectively, nonassertive attitudes and behaviors, and aggressive ones.

The two chapters on nonassertiveness and aggressiveness are intended to describe ways in which individuals typically interact. Although many people believe that they are nonassertive, it has been our experience that in some instances even the most nonassertive person responds aggressively when he feels very safe or very threatened. A nonassertive individual may never ask her husband for help, but she will demand that her ten-year-old child conform to her every desire. The typically aggressive boss may radically change his style of relating and become very nonassertive when his wife calls him at work.

While no one is purely consistent in behavior, we have deliberately separated the nonassertive from the aggressive in order to describe the specific attitudes and behaviors peculiar to each. As you read these two chapters be aware of where and when you have been nonassertive or aggressive. Are there patterns? Are you aggressive with your spouse but not with your boss? Are you nonassertive with your children but not with friends? Do you switch roles from moment to moment?

Following these chapters on nonassertiveness and aggressiveness is a chapter on assertiveness, the style of behaving whose foundation rests on the rights previously discussed. Assertiveness is an alternative to the limitations of nonassertiveness and aggressiveness.

3
A Case Study in Nonassertiveness

Harry and Janet are a married couple in their early thirties. They have two children, ages three and nine. Harry works for an insurance agency and Janet is a housewife. Basically, they are two people who have never learned how to be assertive. They have developed a set of coping behaviors that has permitted them to function with each other within the family system. For instance, Harry knows how to get Janet to do what he wants. If he is aggressive, she will pout and complain, but she will give in. If Janet wants Harry to do something she will ask hesitantly. If he refuses she will remind him of how helpful she is to him and play the martyred housewife, and she usually wins without ever being straightforward. The children are also involved in the game and can manipulate their parents through fear of embarrassment or of a fight.

32 Three Styles of Behaving

In spite of the complicated manipulations in the family system, all parties have a reasonable certainty that this structure works. While situations may arise at home that make both Harry and Janet feel uncomfortable, the results are at least boringly and painfully predictable. But this is not the case when they attempt the same maneuvers outside the family, where interactions are less predictable. They have not had the time with others that they have had together to figure out moves and countermoves. Both live with undue anxiety over interactions with others because of their fear of embarrassment and ultimate rejection by the other person. Both expend considerable energy as they attempt to maintain their interactions and relationships.

Here is a typical day in their lives.

8:00. As Harry leaves for work, Janet asks him to call the bank to rectify a checking account error she made. He grumbles under his breath but agrees.

His feeling: resentful.

As he walks out the door he fumes both at Janet and at his car pool driver who is late again. As he gets into the car he sarcastically asks, "Car die on the way, Charlie?"

His feeling: angry.

As Bob, the other member of the car pool, gets into the car he lights his usual morning cigarette. Harry hates being in the car with smoke, but says nothing. When Bob asks if it bothers him, Harry says, "No, it's all right. I'll just roll down the window."

His feelings: uncomfortable and annoyed.

9:00. By the time he reaches the office, Harry is ready for a fight. Before he even has time to put down his briefcase his receptionist says she wants to take a long lunch hour. Harry knows he can be aggressive with her, so he yells at her to get her to withdraw her request. "Can't you see I'm too busy for such trivial requests?"

His feelings: powerful, aggressive, angry.

10:45. Three staff members are late for the weekly staff meeting. When they arrive Harry ignores the first two and makes a punitive remark to the last person to arrive. "Nice you could join us, Madeline."

His feelings: angry, helpless, out of control.

The staff meeting progresses in its usual one up/one down fashion and Harry makes a hurried retreat for lunch.

12:30. At lunch the waitress brings the wrong salad, but Harry eats it anyway.

His feelings: disgruntled, resigned.

As he leaves he says to the hostess, "The help here sure need to have some brain implants. They can't even bring a customer the right salad."

His feeling: superior for having put her down.

1:30. Harry walks back to work. The heel falls off one of his reheeled shoes. He silently curses, vows never to use that shoe repairman again.

His feelings: humiliated, angry.

2:30. Contracts and work are piling up. Harry wants to ask his secretary to stay late so they can catch up. He walks out of his office twice to her desk but loses his nerve and never says a word.

His feelings: fearful, angry at himself for lacking courage and at her for not volunteering.

3:30. Mr. Dover, the regional boss, stops by Harry's office. Harry feels compelled to invite the boss home for dinner.

His feelings: squeezed—eager to please the boss, but fearful of Janet's reaction.

4:00. Harry calls Janet to tell her his boss is coming home to dinner. He feels scared, but he is determined to win. She complains about how bad her day has been and how hard it will be to fix dinner. He pleads with her and she finally says she will try.

His feelings: relieved, anxious.
Her feelings: resentful, tired.

5:30. Harry and Mr. Dover arrive at Harry and Janet's house for dinner. There is no ice for cocktails. Harry wants to ask his son to go to the corner store and get ice but fears a fight in front of his boss, so he goes himself.

His feelings: angry, helpless.

8:30. Mr. Dover leaves and Harry sits down to watch the newly repaired television. As he turns it on a fuse blows. He tells Janet to replace the fuse, but she pleads that she just sat down and is too tired. Grumbling to himself, Harry hunts for the flashlight, trips over a dog's bone on the basement stairs, and curses all the way to the fuse box.

His feelings: angry, hurt, tired, rejected.

10:30. Harry gets ready for bed, turns out the light, and opens the window, only to hear the

A Case Study in Nonassertiveness 35

neighbor's dog baying at the moon. Harry yells at the dog, slams the window, and wonders why his ulcer is acting up. Harry yells at Janet to put their dog in the kitchen.
His feeling: helpless.
Here is the day from Janet's point of view.

6:45. Janet's day begins as usual. She fixes three separate breakfasts, makes a school lunch for Jimmy, the nine-year-old, feeds the dog and the cat, and watches for the school bus and Harry's ride to work.
Her feelings: tired, unappreciated.

7:15. She asks Jimmy to take out the garbage. He balks. She pleads. He says, "Later," and she takes it out. She rationalizes to herself, "He had to go to school. I have nothing better to do."
Her feeling: helpless.

8:00. Janet asks Harry to call the bank to rectify the checking account error she made. He grumbles. She winces but reminds him of all the things she does for him.
Her feelings: guilty for manipulating him but powerful because he agreed to do something he didn't want to do.

9:00. Jimmy has gone to school, and Janet plans her day. The phone rings. It's Karen, the next-door neighbor who borrows everything. Her vacuum cleaner is broken and she needs to borrow Janet's. Janet says, "I'm planning to clean today."
KAREN: I'll get it when you're through.
JANET: But, I don't know when that will be.

36 Three Styles of Behaving

KAREN: That's OK. Why don't you let me use it first?
JANET: Oh. OK.
Janet's feelings: trapped, helpless.

10:30. Janet goes to pick up Harry's shirts at the laundry. She gives the attendant a ten-dollar bill; he gives her change for a five. Janet gets flustered and can't remember for sure whether she gave him a ten. When he insists it was a five, she leaves, fearful of causing a scene.
Her feelings: stupid, embarrassed.

12:00. Nancy, a community leader, calls to tell Janet that she has been chosen to head up the neighborhood charity drive. Janet tries to refuse, saying, "I don't think I'll have time. I'm thinking about going back to school."
NANCY: Why would you do that? You've already been to college! What would your husband say?
JANET: Oh, I don't know... I'll have to think about the drive.
NANCY: Well, we'll just plan on your participation.
JANET: Well, maybe I can do something on it.
Her feelings: distressed, helpless.

2:30. Janet sits down to watch her favorite television program. Karen comes in.
KAREN: Am I bothering you?
JANET: Yes, but it's all right.
Janet's feeling: resigned.
Karen chatters on and then leaves with the vacuum cleaner.

3:30. Jimmy rushes home from school demanding a ride to football practice. Janet complains, gives the standard lecture, and takes him to practice.

Her feelings: angry, helpless.

4:00. Harry calls to say he is bringing his boss home to dinner.

HARRY: Janet, honey, Mr. Dover is in town and I'm going to bring him home to dinner.

JANET: But we were going to have leftovers.

HARRY: Well, fix that great lasagna.

JANET: But I'm so tired; it's been a rough day.

HARRY: Well, this is really important.

JANET: Well, I'll try.

Her feelings: angry, martyred.

Janet screams at the dog, grabs her younger child, goes to the grocery, comes home, and fixes dinner.

7:30. Dinner is over. Mr. Dover says to Janet, "That was a great meal." Janet says, "Oh, it was nothing. I enjoy doing things like this for my husband."

Her feeling: embarrassed.

8:30. Janet and Harry fight over the fuse. She says, "I'm too tired to go fix the fuse. Besides, I always get confused about which one to change."

Her feeling: satisfied at having played stupid and gotten him to change the fuse.

9:00. Janet tells Harry she is thinking about taking a course at the local university.

HARRY: If that's what you want, go ahead

—as long as it doesn't interfere with your responsibilities around here.
JANET: Oh, it won't. I'll take it while you and the kids are gone.
Her feelings: anxious, hopeful.
10:30. Harry yells at Janet to put the dog in the kitchen. She pretends to be asleep.
Her feeling: satisfied at forcing him to put the dog to bed.

In the preceding case study, Harry and Janet did experience some "successes" during the day. Harry managed on several occasions to stay on top of others by making cutting remarks, being aggressive, and pushing others around. Janet was able to manipulate her husband through making him feel guilty and by passively ignoring him. However, in the end they were both left feeling angry at themselves or others, hurt or humiliated. What a price to pay for getting what they wanted! Each time Harry and Janet were faced with requests or other assertions from others they retreated to past learned behaviors—Harry to aggression or sarcasm, Janet to passivity and manipulation.

Your reaction to this typical day may be that it was excessive, but stop and think: How many times each day do you encounter another person who makes a request of you or refuses to honor your request? At each of these junctures there is an opportunity for your rights to be challenged or infringed on—from a friend's always wanting to bum a cigarette to your spouse's refusal to take time to talk with you. You can increase your success in protecting your rights by learning how to be assertive.

4

Nonassertiveness

For reasons outlined in Part 1, many people respond as if they had no rights at all. The only option open to these individuals seems to be nonassertiveness. They are hurt, frightened, and feel helpless and seem never to be in control of their lives.

In many interactions in our society the nonassertive style has become the norm of acceptable behavior. This nonassertive style, based on years of conditioning, consists of giving up personal rights. Nonassertive people continue to give up personal rights because they believe it is simpler to stay within the system. They believe that this way generates less hassle, less fear of rejection, and greater personal safety. They rely on nonassertive patterns of behavior, letting others choose for them. Thus they are never made to feel guilty for "rocking the boat." However, the nonassertive individual expends much psychological energy, because he is in a continual bind between knowing what he wants and fearing the consequences of asking for it. This fear results in loss of time, energy, and intimacy. For example, Richard's uncle writes to say that he is coming to stay with Richard and his wife for two weeks. Richard does not want his uncle to visit, because it is an inconvenience, but he fears being considered selfish by the rest of his family if he doesn't entertain the uncle. Thus he spends the week before the arrival of the uncle feeling guilty for not wanting the visit, but then responds solicitously to the uncle during his entire stay for fear of having his real feelings show.

By expending energy worrying and behaving in this fashion, Richard got behind in his work at the office, neglected his wife, and was irritable with everyone who came in contact with him. After his uncle finally left, he took to bed with a virus—his way of dissipating the anger he had swallowed about the visit.

A nonassertive person is likely to put others in control of his life and give up part of his individuality because he is unable to ask for what he wants. Although Richard did not want his uncle to visit, he allowed it to happen because he was unable to refuse the request. Fearing rejection or confrontation, he gave up his personal rights by giving in to his uncle's wishes.

The typical nonassertive person placates or appeases others to avoid arguments at all cost. He whines, moans, and complains to others that he never gets any breaks. He says, "Isn't it terrible what happens to me." The whole world is against him. He is likely to look sorrowful and martyred. By allowing others to choose for him he is left feeling hurt, inhibited, anxious, and self-denying. By always acceding to the demands of others, he may not achieve his own goals directly, though he may get what he wants by making others feel guilty or responsible for him.

The nonassertive person, in order to get others to take care of him, may feign illness in order to get what he wants. For example, he uses his migraine headaches as the reason for being unable to take care of himself.

Nonassertive people will typically give in to things that they really don't want to do for fear of hurting someone else's feelings. A typical example is a young married couple who spend every Sunday with their in-laws—not because they want to, but because they believe they will hurt their parents' feelings if they ever say no. Another example is a man who is afraid to say "no" to the next-door neighbor who wants to borrow his garden tools. His response to the man is not to say no. Rather, he says yes, gives an excuse, or possibly even fails to answer the door when the neighbor comes over.

A nonassertive person believes that he has no choices. Rather than identifying the alternatives that are available in every situation, he is likely to respond as if there were but one choice, someone else's. A neighbor asks the nonassertive person to help put up a television antenna. His alternatives are (1) to accept, (2) to refuse, (3) to refuse with a reason such as "I'm afraid of heights," (4) to avoid answering altogether, or (5) to suggest a good repairman. The nonassertive person who simply agrees to help even if he doesn't want to or even if he is afraid of heights is acting as if the neighbor is in control of his world.

A man who never stands up for himself still lives in fear of being rejected by others because each person he relates to has different expectations of him. If he follows the directions of one, he risks rejection from another. To please his boss he may displease his wife. He constantly balances feelings and actions imposed by others. He expends a tremendous amount of time and emotional energy maintaining relationships with all the other persons as he carefully seeks permission from each to exist.

The stance of the nonassertive person makes him look as if he has the weight of the world on his shoulders. He rarely makes direct eye contact with anyone. Instead, he prefers to look at the ground to avoid confrontation. He speaks hesitantly and apologetically and is likely to sit meekly by and wait to be approached. Such is the customer who lets four other people be waited on before the clerk finally approaches him.

Now that we have described what the nonassertive person is like, let's consider three situations and imagine how a nonassertive person might respond in each case. In the first situation, a man bought a coat at a major department store. When he wore it the first time he discovered that it just didn't fit. A nonassertive person would typically keep the coat. He might refuse to return to that store to shop, or he might tell his friends what a terrible salesman the store has. He would very likely put the coat in the back of his closet and never wear it again, all the while hoping it will fit later. At best he might sheepishly return to the store and plead with the salesman to take the coat, but he would hope that the salesman would take the initiative and offer to exchange the coat or give him his money back.

In the second situation, relatives call a woman to say that she and her family are, of course, coming for Thanksgiving dinner at their house. The nonassertive person would acquiesce and then worry about persuading her husband and children to go. Or she might try to forestall the inevitable acceptance by saying that she had to ask her husband what he wanted to do that day.

In the third situation, a husband goes bowling every Saturday afternoon and leaves his wife to watch the children. His wife would like to shop one Saturday but can't find a sitter. The nonassertive wife would not even initiate a request but would watch the children as usual. If it were absolutely necessary that she be gone, the nonassertive person might travel a considerable distance to leave the children with a friend or parent and apologize for bothering them.

In looking at the responses of the nonassertive person to the three situations we can see a pattern. Because it is so difficult for such a person to request or refuse, he hopes and expects that the situation will not arise in which he will have to assert himself. Thus he tries to set up the world in such a way that nothing will be demanded of him. The man in the first situation fails to return the coat for fear of being confronted by the salesperson and told that he cannot exchange it. The woman in the second might deliberately not answer the telephone to avoid having to say no if she knew the time of day that the relatives would be calling. The nonassertive wife in the third situation assumes that her husband would not agree to stay home on Saturday afternoon, so she takes no initiative even to try to change a pattern between them.

When it is necessary for the nonassertive person to respond or to initiate some kind of action, his immediate reaction is to withdraw or acquiesce. He assumes that he could not return the coat, that he or she has no option other than to spend Thanksgiving with the relatives, or that he or she must watch the children or find someone else to take care of them. It is as if his life were out of control and he is helpless to change any situation. His overt response to others is one of self-sacrifice.

When it is absolutely necessary for a nonassertive person to get something he needs, he may think that the only way he can get it is by setting up the situation in such a way that the other person will discern his needs and oblige so he won't have to ask directly. He continually tries to read the mind of the other individual so that he will not offend or have to be assertive. For example, the individual who returns the coat to the department store is hoping the salesperson will offer to take it back. He does not ask the store to take it back but hopes the salesperson will take the initiative. In the family dinner example, the nonassertive person's compliance with the request places her in a bind. She feels guilty for accepting an invitation that neither she nor her family wants and at the same time feels trapped by the old sentiment that families should be together on holidays. In the situation where the spouse is gone every Saturday, the nonassertive wife who wants to be gone would give a bundle of reasons for her change of plans in hopes that one of them will be acceptable and will alleviate her guilt.

Underneath the overt behavior, the nonassertive person may feel hurt and angry that someone would dare to make a request of him and feel helpless and embarrassed to refuse. In extreme cases the nonassertive person avoids everything and everyone. An example would be the worker who comes to her office each morning and immediately phones "dial-a-prayer" to avoid having to interact with anyone.

As a result of continual nonassertive behavior, a person may rationalize his own actions and the actions of other people. He may rationalize that it is his familial obligation to agree to visit the relatives for their sake. Another rationalization would be that the husband who bowls on Saturday works hard all week and therefore needs time to relax; how could the wife be so selfish as to want an afternoon off? In the situation with the coat, the nonassertive person assumes that the salesman couldn't help it if the coat didn't fit. If the salesman doesn't offer to take the coat back, the nonassertive person absolves him of all responsibility and is left feeling hurt, frustrated, and belittled.

In some situations, we have all been nonassertive because it was the easiest course of action, because it was the only alternative that seemed appropriate at the moment, *or* because it was a typical pattern of responding. Take a few minutes and think about situations in which you have been with people who were nonassertive. Think about the situations, the kinds of people who responded nonassertively. Is there a pattern of behavior? Do you know individuals who typically respond nonassertively, people who seem to have no other alternatives?

Now think about some situations in which you have been nonassertive. Write these down, along with your responses—what you said or did not say in each situation. How did you feel?

At the end of Chapter 2 (What Are Your Rights?), you identified three situations in which you were assertive, focusing on how the other person responded. Now think of these situations or others that you remember. Write, to the best of your recollection, what you said or did not say in each situation. How did you feel?

1. What did you say or not say? _____
   _____
   _____
   _____
   How did you feel? _____
   _____
   _____
   _____

2. What did you say or not say? _____
   _____
   _____
   _____
   _____

How did you feel? _____
_____
_____

3. What did you say or not say? _____
_____
_____

What did you feel? _____
_____
_____

5

Aggressiveness

In the cases presented so far, the only alternative to nonassertiveness as a style of interacting, believing, and feeling was aggressiveness. Aggressiveness is getting or obtaining what one wants at the expense of another either by direct intimidation or through more subtle manipulation.

Intimidators act as if they believe that they are surrounded by incompetents and/or potential persecutors. They believe that the only way they can maintain their own rights is by putting others down, by violating others' rights. Typically they get what they want by overtly seizing control over the rights and lives of others. They believe that in order to protect themselves they must act swiftly or risk attack.

The aggressive person's method is primarily to frighten his opponents into submission by blaming them for all that goes awry. To get what he wants, he may ridicule others and leave them feeling hurt, defeated, and humiliated. The aggressive person usually attains his goals, but at the expense of others. In essence, by putting the other person down, he places himself in a one-up position.

The aggressive person continually finds fault with the actions of others and responds as if the whole world were against him. He acts as if his only alternative were to get others before they get him. This aggressive method often works extremely well in limited, impersonal relationships when the aggressor threatens to foreclose on the mortgage, take back the car, complain to the manager, and so on. In such situations the other party gives in out of fear.

An example of an aggressive person's actions would be an angry man's driving into a service station where several cars are waiting to be serviced and demanding that his car be fixed immediately because he has important business to do. Another example of aggressive behavior might come from a hassled passenger trying to get on an overbooked airline flight. In this instance, since he will probably never have contact with the airline agent again, and since the flight is important to him, he humiliates and threatens the agent until he finally is given a seat.

The situations just described are examples of intimidation. The first example characterized the bully, an individual who believes that he should always come first because of who he is or what he represents. The airline passenger's aggressive response, while possibly justified, was still intimidation. Though he would not typically respond in this manner, he will shove rather than be pushed around in emergency situations. Both examples of aggression led to momentary success, but each would probably have negative consequences if the aggressor had to sustain continual contact with the other party involved.

A more common type of intimidation is directed to the manager of a department store by the aggressive person who believes that he was deliberately wronged when the sofa he purchased was delivered damaged. Out of fear of not getting the sofa replaced, the customer verbally attacks and demands immediate attention to the matter while causing a scene in front of other customers. The aggressive person has learned that if he can yell loudly enough and long enough he will gain control of the situation and force people to comply with his demand. The result of this encounter, as well as all others that the aggressive person has, is a tremendous expenditure of energy. He must remain forever guarded and cautious and be prepared to strike at any time. Such a stance of alertness involves a critical supply of energy that must be diverted from other activities.

The intimidator carries himself rigidly, prepared to point his finger, shake a fist, or lash out at anyone who gets in his way. When he is aggressive, his face turns red, his adrenalin level soars, his heart races, and his muscles become taut. The goal of the intimidator is to look and act so fierce that his authority is not questioned; if it were he might crumble or be forced to retreat. Whereas the energy it takes to keep alert and guarded is cognitive energy, the effort required to keep the body readied is physical.

A more subtle form of aggression but one that uses as much, if not more, energy is a manipulative style of aggression. A manipulator, however, is less likely to use physical effort, but relies instead on cognitive energy. The attitudes and behaviors of the manipulative style of aggression are characterized by individuals who get what they want but in a very indirect manner.

Manipulators believe that they can get what they want most effectively if the other person is tricked, conned, or duped into believeing that he *should* comply. The manipulator may view people as pawns who can readily be used for his own purposes. Unlike the intimidator, the manipulator fears being direct and thus risking confrontation or rejection, so he approaches situations indirectly.

For example, a secretary who fears a confrontation if she refuses to work late instead sabotages her boss's project by not completing the work properly. Another example of a manipulator is a door-to-door salesman who cons a homeowner into believing he needs the salesman's product. Then there is the mother who plays on the sympathy of her children when they refuse to eat something by saying, "Think of all the starving children in the world. They would love to eat spinach."

All these are examples of manipulation. The secretary, who can be characterized as a "revenger," fears refusing a request but gets even in a passively aggressive manner by failing to finish the job correctly. If confronted, she will complain that she could have done the work correctly if she had not been so tired. The salesman's pitch is designed to manipulate the potential customer into purchasing his product. Thus he may say, "Which one would you like?" rather than directly asking the customer to purchase from him.

Another example of manipulative behavior can occur when a woman asks her husband whether they can budget money for a new living room chair. When asked, her husband may resent the request and punish his wife by putting her down verbally. He may imply that the chair should be low on their list of priorities, that she doesn't know the value of money, and so on. The wife still may get what she wants, however, because, if she is a manipulator, she has already learned an intricate system of manipulation to deal with her husband. It is true that he has refused her request to set aside money for the new chair, but she will retaliate. She may complain in front of company about the old frayed chair, or ask a guest not to sit there because the springs are worn out. Any variation on that theme is a manipulation designed to get a new chair without changing the basic marital system already in operation.

There are many kinds of manipulation: appeals to the emotions, induction of guilt, and threats of physical violence or rejection. The most obvious manipulation is the threat of physical harm. A more subtle but equally important one is the threat of rejection. It has been shown that people will do almost anything to avoid being rejected. The common phrase that triggers this fear is "If you love me, you'll..." Underlying this statement is the manipulative message, "*I* won't love *you* if you don't do it."

A special set of manipulative behaviors often occurs in sexual relationships in which each person fears direct refusal (or in some cases assent) and thus hopes his partner will read his mind and know what he really wants. Such a situation occurs between the couple in our earlier case study when Harry wants to have sex and is afraid Janet will refuse him. Thus he makes indirect overtures to her. She knows what he wants but fears appearing too eager, so she ignores or refuses his initial advances. Like two stalking animals they circle and skirt the issue of sex until Harry gives up or Janet gives in or vice versa.

The manipulator uses a variety of behaviors to cover his actions. Pleading, pouting, avoiding eye contact, and looking pathetic, helpless, coy, or cunning are all examples of manipulative postures. There are myriad possibilities and each person has discovered his own style of indirectness. The energy it takes to be indirect and manipulative is expended at the thought level as the manipulator carefully plots his or her course of action. After careful scrutiny of the situation and consideration of possible consequences, the plan must then be implemented. The anxiety generated in preparing and implementing an indirect posture requires energy that could be utilized in more productive ways.

Persons who use both styles of aggressiveness—intimidation and manipulation—suffer because of their inability to deal effectively with others. They expend physical, emotional, and cognitive energy and pay a great price for it. The energy they use could be put to more effective use in other areas of their lives for their own pleasure.

Now that we have examined how the aggressive person typically responds, let's return to the situations described in Chapter 4 and show how an aggressive person would respond in each one.

First was the man who bought a coat and discovered that it didn't fit. The aggressive intimidator storms angrily back into the store and demands to see the manager or the salesman. He might seek out the person who sold him the coat, make a scene, and humiliate the salesman. He gives no option and attacks directly.

Second was the phone call from relatives insisting that the family come for Thanksgiving dinner. The aggressive person would have gotten angry initially, would have found fault with the person for having dared assume he would come, and would probably have demanded to know why this person takes his presence for granted. His statement might be, "What made you think we would drive all the way just for one day?" He places the responsibility on the other person for lacking enough sense to know that he had no intentions of going. He will refuse to go on any account and will punish the individual with a guilt-inducing lecture about being considerate of others' feelings.

In the third situation the husband routinely goes off to bowl on Saturday afternoon, so the wife must watch the children. The intimidator would never have let the situation get started in the first place. She would have demanded that he stay home and watch the children because she had been home with them all week. If indeed the husband wanted to be gone on a Saturday she would be most likely to set up an angry scene and demand that her Saturdays were her free time away from the children. The demand would be intended to attack and humiliate the husband to the point that, if he were to go, he would feel guilty about going.

Looking at the three situations and the responses of an intimidator, we again see a pattern emerge. The intimidator expects other people to know better than to ask a favor of him and at the same time is sure that he has the right to demand, not request, that things be done *for* him. He clearly places the responsibility on the other person in that he expects him never to ask, but always to give him exactly what he wants. His actions are to attack, refuse, or become hostile. Aggressive people get what they want, but they pay in interpersonal relationships. They limit their relationships. Negotiations with aggressive persons are not feasible. They demand; they don't request. They come across as nonforgiving and nonforgetting. Underneath their attack is a feeling of anger, an awareness of having to get the other person before they are gotten themselves. They are left feeling superior and triumphant, for there is a real, if short-lived, triumph in the one-up kind of position. They are likely to attack the character rather than the action of another individual when making a demand. Each of us has encountered aggressive people as we have described them. They usually make us feel uncomfortable and uneasy with their demands.

The manipulator, returning the coat to the department store, seeks out a different salesperson and says sadly, "I really thought I could count on the other salesman to help me select such an important thing as a coat. I guess you salespeople are just too anxious to make a sale these days." Although the salesman may cover for his co-worker, he is likely to apologize on behalf of the store, take back the coat, and agree to be of assistance in every way he can.

When the manipulator receives the telephone call from her relatives, she enthusiastically agrees to come for Thanksgiving, asks what she can bring, and says, "It will be wonderful to see you again!" However, on Thanksgiving Day, she just happens to be ill and is forced to call the relatives and say, "We looked forward to coming so much, but I'm just not feeling well."

In the third situation the manipulator might say as her spouse left the house, "Honey, you have a wonderful time. I'll stay here and iron your shirts and I'll just tell Dr. Wilson that he can run these tests on me another day." The husband, unless he is extremely sensitive to the ploy, will be left feeling so guilty that he will at least stop and consider what she has said and may not go at all, particularly after that line about the medical tests!

Think for a minute about the kind of people you've known who have responded aggressively, as either intimidators or manipulators. Do you see a pattern in their behaviors? Look at the kinds of interactions *you* have had with people. Have you used excuses or acted coy? Think of two incidents in which you either have been the recipient of an aggressive response or have been the aggressor. Write the situation along with the way you responded.

1. When you were aggressive: _____
   _____
   _____

   How did you feel? _____
   _____
   _____

2. When you were a recipient of an aggressive attack: _____
   _____
   _____

   How did you feel? _____
   _____
   _____

6
Assertiveness

In contrast to the nonassertive or aggressive behavior described in the previous chapters and in the case study of Harry and Janet, you have an alternative. Earlier we discussed the rights and attitudes of an assertive individual. Although attitudes are a crucial part of being assertive, an equivalent aspect of assertiveness is the behavior or actions that match those attitudes. All of the assertive behaviors discussed in the present chapter logically follow from the three basic rights discussed earlier (to refuse, to rectify a wrong, and to request).

The purpose of this chapter is to provide you with a clear description of how an assertive person thinks, feels, and acts. When you have finished reading this chapter, *you* should be able to identify and understand the actions of an assertive person.

An assertive person, in contrast to the nonassertive or aggressive person, knows his rights and is able to act on them. He is also aware of other people's rights. Our definition of an assertive person is one who straightforwardly enhances his own position and obtains his own desired personal goals, but not at the expense of another person. He is fully able to express his feelings and emotions but also allows others to do the same. Both he and the people he relates to can feel good about themselves and each other. Because he is aware of his rights and choices, he can frequently attain his goals. In assertive interactions both parties are self-enhanced, which is an important aspect of assertive behavior. Everyone has the right to be an individual and to work toward his desired goals while respecting the rights of the persons receiving his communications.

For example, in an assertive relationship, you may ask to borrow a friend's car any time but the owner can also refuse at any time. You ask based on your needs and desires but also recognize that the owner will respond to you based on his own needs and desires. Neither your self-worth nor his is contingent on his acceptance or rejection of your request.

The most important characteristic of an assertive person is his awareness of himself in relation to the world around him. Through this self-awareness, which includes his thoughts and feelings as well as his behavior, he comes to realize his own uniqueness. Because he understands himself better than anyone else he looks first to himself for direction and relies on his own good judgment when making decisions. An assertive person may request information or suggestions from other people but before taking action he makes a conscious choice among the alternatives. He knows he is ultimately responsible for his decision regardless of the circumstances. As a result of believing in himself, he takes seriously his own thoughts and feelings. In other words, he takes himself seriously. Because an assertive person values himself he is able to trust his judgment in each situation. He is different from nonassertive people who take others seriously but not themselves and who trust others' judgment rather than their own.

The assertive person has learned that if he stops and pauses to listen to himself he will come up with the best solution for himself without hurting the other person. On the other hand an aggressive person listens only to himself, often out of fear that the other person might take advantage of him. The assertive person trusts that if he listens to his own thoughts and feelings he will act in a way that is in his best interests without taking undue advantage of others.

As a result of identifying his own thoughts and feelings he is able to set limits and goals for himself. He sets limits by acting on his rights to refuse and to rectify.

An example of setting limits through the right to refuse is when out-of-town guests call to say they're just outside of town and hint that they would like to spend the night. An assertive person simply gives a clear statement that it is inconvenient to have house guests that evening.

Another example is when you return your car radio to the dealer because the push buttons don't work properly. Even though he told you he couldn't do anything about the push buttons, you request that a different radio be put in.

After having waited all day for the furnace repairman to make his promised call on Saturday, the assertive person calls to rectify the wrong that has been done. When the repairman apologizes and offers to come immediately, the assertive person insists on setting the appointment according to his or her schedule, which may mean that the repairman come in the evening.

A final example of rectifying a wrong is when you sell your neighbor a snow blower, and he initially pays you one-half of the amount due. After a reasonable period of time, you contact the neighbor and ask for payment of the remaining amount.

The preceding instances of the right to refuse and to rectify came as results of infringements on the limits set by an assertive person. The assertive person did not want overnight guests dropping in unexpectedly, did not want a car radio that didn't function properly, did not want the furnace fixed at an unreasonable time, and did want the money owed for the snow blower from the neighbor. An assertive person knows that his rights have been infringed because of the way he feels. When he feels angry, put upon, hasseled, depressed, or irritated, his limits are being tested.

You also know that your rights have been infringed upon if you think that, on the basis of your newly acquired rights, you want your limits to be different. However, it is important to understand that limits are not rigid; they are flexible and can be modified as the assertive person desires. It might have been appropriate to suggest a motel for the unexpected guests and meet them for breakfast, to return at a more convenient time to have the radio exchanged, to suggest that the repairman select one of several possible times, and to accept several small payments from the neighbor until the money was repaid.

The assertive person, further, is an individual who takes responsibility for himself. This means that prior to taking assertive action he considers all options and makes his decision a conscious choice based on the best option. This does not imply, however, that he is superindependent or that he is infallible. Just as it is unwise to be superdependent, it is also unwise to be completely independent.

The power of the assertive individual lies in his ability to know when to ask for support and assistance. He is cognizant of the limits of his knowledge and ability, thus enabling him to request help in making choices. He still accepts responsibility for himself even when he asks for help. He is able to change his mind and to make mistakes.

When an assertive person makes a request, he is clearly stating his goal for himself. He is willing to ask outright for his most desired goal. If he needs to borrow a hundred dollars, he will ask for a hundred dollars. A nonassertive person, in contrast, would hedge, explaining why he needs to borrow, but probably not asking for all that he needs in the hope that the loaner will offer to give him the money.

The assertive person may not always get everything that he wants or needs, but he has the satisfaction of knowing that he made the request directly regardless of the outcome. Moreover, because he has thought out his precise needs and asked directly he is more likely to get what he wants. In addition, his careful consideration of his needs leads him to consider other options if his request is refused. In summary, the assertive person uses limits to establish the boundaries around himself in order to prevent personal infringement, while he establishes goals to extend his powers of request.

Setting limits and goals does not preclude an awareness of the feelings of others. Because the assertive person is aware of his own rights he is equally aware of the rights of others and he respects them. For example, imagine that you decide not to visit your family for the holidays but to go skiing instead. When you make your announcement, your mother is very disappointed because your not being there will spoil a family tradition. The assertive person is aware of and empathizes with his mother's disappointment, and communicates that awareness to her, but at the same time he respects his own feelings and sticks by his decision. He is aware of the danger that he will be made to feel responsible for his mother and thus feel guilty. He is careful not to lose sight of himself by falling prey to others' expectations.

The assertive person knows that he makes the ultimate decision regarding how he feels. He knows that you can say anything you want to him but only he is responsible for determining how he feels and how he reacts to what you have said. The assertive person knows that other people do not cause him to feel bad. He does that to himself, by the manner in which he interprets what is said.

Looking now at the three situations previously discussed in reference to nonassertive people and aggressive people, we can compare how the assertive person might respond in each situation. In the case of the coat that didn't fit, an assertive person would take the coat back, seek out the salesman who sold it to him, and ask to speak with him for a moment. His statement to the salesman might be, "I know it's important to you to make a sale, but this coat you sold me yesterday just doesn't fit; I want to exchange it." Notice first of all that he communicated how he thought the salesman was feeling; second, he communicated in a specific, straightforward manner his conflict with the salesman's feelings; and third, he communicated very specifically what he wanted to happen—that he wanted to exchange the coat. In this statement there is little danger of a misunderstanding.

In the case of the relatives calling about Thanksgiving dinner, the assertive person would express appreciation at having been invited, but would politely refuse if he or she did not wish to accept. He might choose to give an explanation if he believed it was important that he do so. Otherwise, a firm, polite refusal would be sufficient.

In the final case of the husband who routinely bowls every Saturday afternoon, the assertive spouse might say, "I know you enjoy your game every Saturday, but I have something important that I need to do this week, so I'd like very much for you to watch the children."

This chapter has identified the ways an assertive person feels, thinks, and acts. Assertiveness is based upon the idea that each person has certain personal rights. By knowing these rights and by beginning to believe, and subsequently, to adopt these attitudes for yourself, the process of becoming more assertive has begun.

Part 3

A Verbal Response Model of Assertiveness

It's nice to know that you have choices, but until you choose to act on them the choices are really not yours. The purpose of this section is to provide guidelines for responding in a specified way to a variety of situations. This method of responding, which has three specific parts, or components, can be regarded as a verbal response model of assertiveness. In order to provide the reader with a clear understanding of this model, each component will be presented individually and then the three will be combined into a full response. The first part of the assertive response might be called the empathy statement—that is, a statement that shows your ability to see the situation through the other person's eyes. The second part takes into consideration your expectations or goals and your perception of what is happening. It usually points out a conflict between what you wanted to happen and what is actually happening. The third part is an action statement, an explanation of what you want to happen, given the conflict that you perceive.

Here is an example of the model. Henry, a friend of yours, stops by frequently to chat on his way home from work. This is a time when you like to relax without entertaining. What would you do if you wanted this practice to stop? You might say, "Henry, I know you enjoy visiting us, but when I first get home I like to be alone with my family. I'd like for us to arrange another time that's more convenient for both of us for you to visit."

The first part of the response expressed empathy by accurately reflecting your understanding of how Henry was feeling. You communicated an understanding that he was enjoying himself. The empathy statement was: "I know you enjoy visiting us..."

The second part of the response is the conflict statement. It describes in a specific, precise manner the conflict between what you want and what is actually occurring: "...but when I first get home I like to be alone with my family." With this statement you let the other person know what you see as a conflict between your desired goal and the current state of affairs.

The action statement lets the other person know what you want: "I'd like for us to arrange another time that's more convenient for both of us for you to visit." Once again, this is a concise, direct statement of how you want to achieve your goal to be alone with your family.

In summary, then, you might think of the model in terms of the following equation:

Empathy + Conflict + Action = Assertion

Empathy is understanding another person's situation; the conflict statement describes the discrepancy between what you want to happen and what is occurring; and the action statement is a description of what you want to happen now. Together the three components make up an assertive statement.

Another way to describe the model is to regard empathy, conflict, and action from a slightly different perspective. From your point of view, the empathy part of an assertive response is a statement of *where the other person is*. Conflict could be described as *where you are,* how you perceive the situation right now. (A conflict statement almost always begins with the word *but*:—"but now I've changed my mind," "but we can't come next weekend," "but I won't give it to you.")

The action statement is another way of stating *what's to be done.* These statements usually begin with the implied word *therefore:* "[therefore] I want to exchange this," "[therefore] I'd like to see you some other time," "[therefore] you will have to do without my vacuum cleaner."

7
Empathy

The first element of the assertive response is the statement of empathy—a recognition of what the other person is feeling. One of the most important ingredients of a communication between you and another individual is the ability to let that person know you understand his point of view. We know that people who are high in empathic understanding are the most successful in their communications with other people because they are able to let the other individual know that they genuinely understand what he is saying. In order to respond accurately to another person you must learn to discriminate, to discern what he is saying and feeling. The easiest way to identify how another person feels is to imagine yourself in his situation. In order to help you learn to discern what another person may be feeling, you are asked to complete some exercises. These exercises will help you master the first segment of the assertive response—namely, the empathy statement.

The following are examples of interpersonal interactions in which you might find yourself. Read each vignette and write down what you think *the other person* might be feeling. Be concise and try to use only one or two words.

> *Example 1*: You are in line to see a movie when four people break in line in front of you. There is a good chance that the movie will be sold out, as it is very popular.

Write some words that might describe how the four people who broke in line are feeling: _____

_____

Here are some words that you might have used to describe their feelings: *eager, excited, rushed, anxious, hurried, nervous, tense.* Compare your words with the words suggested here. Did you capture what the four people themselves might be feeling? Now complete the following examples in the same manner.

> *Example 2*: An acquaintance is moving to a new apartment. She asks if you would help her move this weekend. You are looking forward to just relaxing and reading a good book.

Now write some words that might describe how *your acquaintance* might be feeling about moving:

_____

_____

Empathy 73

Some words that might describe her feelings are *scared, anxious, excited, overworked, rushed.*

Example 3: You have spent about half an hour with a car salesman. You think that you might like a particular car, but before you can really decide the salesman is writing up the contract. On second thought, you decide that you really do not want the car, but he has already presented you with the contract to sign.

Write some words that might describe how *the car salesman* is feeling: _____

_____

The car salesman might be feeling eager, excited, pressured.

Example 4: You are standing near a cash register in a store waiting to pay for some clothes you want to buy. Several other people who came to the cash register after you did are being waited on first by the saleslady. You are getting tired of waiting.

Write some words that might describe what *the saleslady* is feeling: _____

_____

Words such as *hassled, busy, unaware, rushed,* or *overworked* would be appropriate to describe how the saleslady might be feeling.

Example 5: Your mother has just accused you of eating the can of olives that she was planning to use for her party. You didn't do it.

74 A Verbal Response Model of Assertiveness

Write some words that might describe how *your mother* is feeling: _____

_____

She might be feeling anxious about entertaining, angry, disappointed, upset, furious.

> *Example 6*: You are trying to go to sleep but the noise from your neighbor's party is preventing you from doing so.

Write some words that describe how *your neighbor* might be feeling: _____

_____

She might be feeling happy, excited, joyful.

> *Example 7*: Your father calls on the telephone to chat with you since he hasn't heard from you for awhile. You are just leaving the house to go to the dry cleaners before they close for the day.

Write some words that describe how *your father* might be feeling: _____

_____

He might be feeling lonely, out of contact, happy, concerned.

> *Example 8*: You bought a CB radio from a local dealer who assured you that it would fit your foreign car. After attempting to install it, you realize that it won't fit. You want your money back, but the dealer refuses and only offers you credit on another radio.

Write some words that might describe how the *radio dealer* might be feeling: _____

_____

He might be feeling pressured, annoyed, exasperated, angry.

Now that you have identified how the other person in the examples might be feeling, select what you think is the most important "feeling" word. Include this "feeling" word in the following phrase: "I realize that you are—"

For example: "I realize that you are eager to see the movie," or "I realize that you are anxious about moving this weekend." These are examples of good empathy statements that communicate your understanding of how the other person might be feeling.

You can use a variety of phrases to introduce an empathy statement, such as "I know," "I understand that," "I can see that." Exactly what you say will depend on how well you know the other person and the formality of the situation.

Now refer to each example and write an empathy statement for each one.

Example 1: _____

_____

Example 2: _____

_____

Example 3: _____

_____

Example 4: _____

_____

Example 5: _____

_____

By using an empathy statement at the beginning of an assertive response, you indicate to the other person that you understand him or hear him. The effect of the empathy statement on the other person is that it increases the likelihood of his responding favorably to the remainder of your assertive statement. If he feels heard, he may be more likely to hear *you*. By being empathic with someone, you decrease the possible consequences of being assertive.

8
Conflict

This chapter concentrates on the second part of the assertive response, the conflict statement. Remember the model: Empathy + Conflict + Action = Assertion. In communicating with another individual, you must not only be able to let him know that you understand what he is feeling or thinking, but you must also be aware of how you feel and how you perceive the situation. The conflict statement is a statement of the discrepancy, as you perceive it, between what you want and what is happening to you at the moment. Another way of thinking about the conflict statement is to ask yourself, "What is my goal? What do I want to happen?" Then, "How is that goal in conflict with what is happening to me right now?"

Let us now turn to the same examples and identify what would be your goal in each example.

78 A Verbal Response Model of Assertiveness

Example 1: You are in line to see a movie when four people break in line in front of you. There is a good chance that the movie will be sold out, as it is very popular.

What would be your goal? Your goal in this situation would be to see the movie. Now complete the rest of the examples in the same manner.

Example 2: An acquaintance is moving to a new apartment. She asks you if you would help her move this weekend. You are looking forward to just relaxing and reading a good book.

What is your goal? Your goal is to relax and read a good book.

Example 3: You have spent about half an hour with a car salesman. You think that you might like a particular car, but before you can really decide the salesman is writing up the contract. On second thought, you decide that you really do not want the car, but he has already presented you with the contract to sign.

What is your goal? Your goal is to take time to make your decision.

Example 4: You are standing near a cash register in a store waiting to pay for some clothes you want to buy. Several other people who came to the cash register after you did are being waited on first by the saleslady. You are getting tired of waiting.

What is your goal? Your goal is to purchase the clothes.

Example 5: Your mother has just accused you of eating the can of olives that she was planning to use for her party. You didn't do it.
What is your goal? Your goal is to set the record straight that you did not eat the olives.

Now that you have identified your goal in a situation, you are in a position to be aware of how that goal is in conflict with the events that are occurring. Your awareness of this difference is communicated in the conflict statement. An easy way to begin a conflict statement is with the word *but*. This will be illustrated in the first example.

Example 1: You are in line to see a movie when four people break in line in front of you. There is a good chance that the movie will be sold out, as it is very popular.
Your goal is to see the movie, but now that the people have broken in line in front of you, there is a possibility that you will not obtain your goal. So you communicate your perception of the conflict. Write a conflict statement beginning with the word *but*. _____

_____

Here are some possible responses. "But we were ahead of you." "But breaking in line isn't fair to the rest of us." "But we've been waiting for a long time."

With your goal in mind, write a conflict statement for the rest of the examples.

80 A Verbal Response Model of Assertiveness

Example 2: An acquaintance is moving to a new apartment. She asks you if you would help her move this weekend. You are looking forward to just relaxing and reading a good book. (Remember, your goal was to relax this weekend; the conflict was a request for you to help her move.)
Write a conflict statement. _____
_____

Example 3: You have spent about half an hour with a car salesman. You think that you might like a particular car, but before you can really decide the salesman is writing up the contract. On second thought, you decide that you really do not want the car, but he has already presented you with the contract to sign.
Now write a conflict statement. _____
_____

Example 4: You are standing near a cash register in a store waiting to pay for some clothes you want to buy. Several other people who came to the cash register after you did are being waited on first by the saleslady. You are getting tired of waiting.
Now write a conflict statement for this example.
_____
_____
_____
_____

Conflict 81

Example 5: Your mother has just accused you of eating the can of olives that she was planning to use for her party. You didn't do it.
Write a conflict statement for this example.

_____
_____
_____

Example 6: You are trying to go to sleep but the noise from your neighbor's party is preventing you from doing so.
Write a conflict statement for this example.

_____
_____
_____

Example 7: Your father calls on the telephone to chat with you since he hasn't heard from you for awhile. You are just leaving the house to go to the dry cleaners before they close for the day.
Write a conflict statement for this example.

_____
_____
_____
_____
_____

Example 8: You bought a CB radio from a local dealer who assured you that it would fit your foreign car. After attempting to put it in the car you realize that it won't fit. You want your money back, but he only offers you credit on another radio.

Write a conflict statement for this example.

_____
_____
_____

In summary, then, the conflict portion of the assertive response sets the scene for what you want to have happen by identifying the discrepancy between your goal and the actual situation. If your goals were already being met, there would be no reason to be assertive, but since they are in some way being restricted or unmet, you are faced with a conflict. Thus, by verbalizing the conflict, you can then state how you want the situation to change.

9
Action

The third, or action, phase of the assertive statement clarifies what action you want accomplished so that you may achieve your goal. In the assertive response you can think of the action statement as being the "therefore" statement. It can begin with the word *therefore, so,* or *and,* or it can have no introductory word. In the first example your action statement to the four people might be "... therefore, please go to the end of the line" or "... so please move."

In the second example, an acquaintance wanted you to help her move. Write an action statement for this example. _____
_____
_____

84 A Verbal Response Model of Assertiveness

In the third example, a salesman was trying to sell you a car. Your action statement to him might be: _____

_____

In the fourth example, the saleslady ignored you. What is your action statement to her?

_____

In the fifth example, your mother accused you of eating the olives. What is your action statement to her? _____

_____

In the sixth example, the noise from the party was keeping you awake. Your action statement to him might be: _____

_____

In the seventh example, your father called you to chat. Your action statement to him might be:

_____

In the final example, you bought the CB radio from the salesman that didn't fit. Your action statement to him might be: _____

_____

For each of the eight situations you have now written an empathy statement, a conflict statement, and an action statement to make an assertive response that includes consideration of the feelings of the other individual, your awareness of the conflict between your goal and the present situation, and a statement of what you want to happen. Now write down your complete assertive response to each of the examples:

Example 1: _____

Example 2: _____

Example 3: _____

Example 4: _____

Example 5: _____

Example 6: _____

Example 7: _____

Example 8: _____

Following are some examples of good assertive responses to these eight situations.
1. "I realize that you're excited about seeing the movie, but we were here before you, so please get in line behind me."
    "I can see that you are anxious to see the movie, but we've been waiting in line for half an hour; therefore, please go to the end of the line."
2. "I can understand that you are overworked and need help moving, but I had planned to spend this weekend alone; therefore, I am unwilling to help you move."
    "I know that you are excited about moving this weekend, but I have other plans, so I won't be able to help you this time."
3. "I know you want to make this sale, but I want more time to make my decision, so I won't sign the contract right now."
    "I can see you feel pressured to make this sale, but I don't feel like I have had enough time to consider the alternatives; therefore, I am unwilling to sign right now."
4. "I realize that you're busy, but I was here before these other customers. Please wait on me next."
    "I know that it's important for you to please your customers, and I was here ahead of these other people, so please wait on me now."
5. "Mom, I can see how angry you are, but I didn't eat the olives, so please don't blame me for something that I didn't do."
    "Mom, I know that you are upset with me, but I didn't eat the olives, so please don't take your anger out on me."

6. "I know that you are probably unaware of the noise that your group is making, but I am trying to sleep, so please ask your guests to hold the noise down."

"I can hear that you are having a great time over there, but I have to get up early in the morning and am trying to sleep, so please ask your friends to lower the noise level."

7. "Dad, I know that you are lonely and want to talk, but I was just leaving for the dry cleaners before it closes; therefore, I'll call you back as soon as I return."

"Dad, I know that you are excited about finally getting in touch with me, but I was just leaving. I will be home after seven this evening if you could call back then please."

8. "I know that it's your policy not to make cash refunds, but I am unhappy with the radio and don't believe that another one will meet my needs; therefore, I would like my money refunded."

"I understand that you are very busy right now, but I am unhappy with this radio and want my money back."

Here are several new situations. Following each one are four typical responses: two aggressive, one nonassertive, and one assertive. Compare the three styles of responding.

Situation 1: A friend borrowed your car for the evening and returned it without replacing the gas he used.

   a. Aggressive—indirect: "You sure must have driven around a lot last night."

b. Aggressive—direct: "What kind of a friend are you to borrow my car and bring it back with the tank empty?"

c. Nonassertive: (You say nothing to your friend but complain to your wife about the empty tank.)

d. Assertive: "I realize it probably slipped your mind, but when I loaned you my car the tank was full, and now it's empty. I'd like you to fill it up."

Situation 2: A wife has taken a full-time job and needs her husband to share in the responsibility for preparing evening meals.

a. Aggressive—indirect: "I'd love to cook dinner tonight, but since I have to do everything myself and work too, I just don't feel up to it."

b. Aggressive—direct: "How come I have to do everything for you and you don't do anything to help me out?"

c. Nonassertive: (The wife continues to do all chores, plus her job, and gets up earlier.)

d. Assertive: "I know you enjoy being able to relax when you come home, but on the evenings I work late everyone gets hungry. When you get home first will you take responsibility for starting dinner?"

Situation 3: Your supervisor has just told you that you are being promoted and transferred out of state. You do not want to move.

a. Aggressive—indirect: "I'd really appreciate that transfer if it weren't for my wife and kids. They couldn't move . . ."

b. Aggressive—direct: "Look, sport. I've moved every year for the past eight. No one's going to get me out of here again!"

c. Nonassertive: (You call your wife and say, "Guess what. We've been transferred to the Midwest with a huge promotion." You say to your boss, "That's nice; how soon do you need for me to go?")

d. Assertive: "I know it's important for you to have one of your trainees promoted, but I don't want to leave my present position because I enjoy my job and responsibilities, so I would like to turn down the promotion."

Situation 4: Two months have passed since you were promised a new refrigerator for your apartment. You call the manager.

a. Aggressive—indirect: "I realize it's only been two months since you promised us the refrigerator, and I wouldn't be bothering you now, but this is the sixth consecutive week that the milk has spoiled."

b. Aggressive—direct: "All you landlords are alike—rip-off artists. You promised me a new refrigerator two months ago and I demand that it be replaced today or you will hear from my lawyer."

c. Nonaggressive: (You do nothing and complain to the neighbors about poor service.)

d. Assertive: "I know that you may have forgotten, but we agreed when I moved in that you would replace the faulty refrigerator in my apartment. Would you please tell me precisely when the refrigerator will be delivered?"

10
A Case Study in Assertiveness

The following is a typical day with Harry and Janet as it might be if they were assertive with each other and with those around them.

8:00. As Harry leaves for work Janet asks him to call the bank to rectify a checking account error she made.

HARRY (*appreciating Janet's feelings*): Janet, I know calls like that upset you, but I think since you made the error it's your responsibility to take care of it. I'd like you to call.

JANET: You're right. I'll accept the responsibility.

Janet's feelings: anxious over having to make the call, but pleased with herself.

As he gets into the car, Harry says to the car pool driver who is often late, "Charlie, I know you don't mean to be late every morning, but it really bothers me to have to worry about being late for work. I'd appreciate it if you'd make arrangements to be on time."

Harry's feelings: good about himself, no longer angry at Charlie.

Bob gets into the car and lights up a cigarette and asks his usual question, "Does the smoke bother you?"

HARRY: Well, yes. I know you enjoy your morning cigarette, but it *is* bothering me. How about either putting it out or opening the window on your side so the smoke will go that way?

BOB: Sure.

Harry's feeling: satisfied.

9:00. As Harry walks in the door of his office, the receptionist requests a long lunch hour.

HARRY: Natalie, I'm sure you must have a good reason for wanting a long lunch hour, but I'm not sure how the workload will be going today. We'll have to discuss it later.

NATALIE: But I have to know now!

HARRY: I can see it's important to you, but I haven't even seen my work schedule yet. I'll talk with you again in about an hour.

NATALIE: Oh, OK.

10:45. Three staff members are late for the staff meeting. When they arrive Harry acknowledges the presence of each one.

HARRY: I'm certain you all have good reasons for being late, but I'm running a very tight schedule and would appreciate your prompt attendance in the future.

MADELINE: But I have another meeting at 9:30, and I can't guarantee that I can be on time.

HARRY: I can appreciate your situation, but this is the time we agreed on. I have to expect you to be here unless you have suggestions for a different time.

MADELINE: I know we agreed on this time, but eleven o'clock would be a much better starting time for me. Could we change it?

HARRY: I don't see why not if all of us agree. What about the rest of you?

All agree and the meeting proceeds.

Harry's feeling: pleased.

12:30. At lunch the waitress brings the wrong salad. Harry gets her attention and says: "I know you're busy, but you brought me a chef salad when I ordered a Waldorf. Would you bring me the Waldorf salad, please?"

Harry's feeling: satisfied.

1:30. Harry walks back to work. The heel falls off one of his reheeled shoes. Annoyed, he makes a mental note to stop by the shoe repair shop on the way home and ask that the heels be put on properly.

Harry's feeling: annoyed, but pleased with himself for planning appropriate action.

2:30. Contracts and work are piling up. Harry wants to ask his secretary to stay late so they can catch up.

HARRY: Nancy, I know this is unexpected, but I need to get the Gordon contracts out by nine tomorrow morning. Will you stay late to finish them?

NANCY: I know those are important, but I've already made plans, so I won't be able to stay very long.

HARRY: I'm sure your plans are important, but those contracts have to be ready by nine. Is there some other way we can have them ready?

NANCY: I can't stay this evening, but I'll be willing to come in early tomorrow to finish up.

HARRY: That's fine with me as long as they get done.

Harry's feelings: relieved and satisfied.

3:30. Mr. Dover, the regional boss, stops by Harry's office. After they discuss business Harry calls Janet.

HARRY: Janet, I know this is short notice, but Mr. Dover is in town and I'd like to bring him home for dinner tonight.

JANET: Harry, I know Mr. Dover would really appreciate a home-cooked meal, but I've been busy all day and I'm not up to fixing a company meal now. He'll have to take a rain check.

HARRY: I know it's late, but I really want Mr. Dover to meet you. Will you please make this exception?

JANET: Honey, I'm quite willing to have Mr. Dover come by for cocktails, but dinner is out. If you want to have dinner, you can take the three of us out to eat.

HARRY: OK, that's worth it. We'll see you about 5:30.

Harry's feelings: relieved and satisfied.

5:30. Harry and Mr. Dover arrive. There is no ice in the house. Harry says to his son, "I know you just got home from football practice, but I need a favor. Will you go to the corner store and get a bag of ice?"

JIMMY: Oh gee, Dad. I don't want to.

HARRY: I'm sure you don't want to, but it would really help me, so please go on and do it.

JIMMY: Ah, OK.

Harry's feeling: satisfied.

8:30. Harry and Janet return home after dropping Mr. Dover off after dinner. Harry turns on the newly repaired television, and immediately a fuse blows.

HARRY: Janet, will you please fix the fuse?

JANET: I'm exhausted, and I really don't want to rumble around in the basement to find a fuse. You do it.

HARRY: OK. I'll do it if you'll put the dog to bed.

JANET: Sure.

Harry's and Janet's feelings: satisfied and treated fairly.

10:30. Harry gets ready for bed, turns out the light, and opens the window, only to hear the neighbor's dog baying at the moon. Harry picks up the telephone, calls his neighbor and says, "Sam, I know it's late but will you please quiet your dog. We're trying to sleep. Thanks."

Janet's day begins differently now also.

6:45. She prepares one breakfast for her family and makes a lunch for Jimmy. Jimmy also feeds the dog and cat, and he and Harry now take responsibility for their own bus and car pool rides.

7:15. Janet says to Jimmy, "I know you don't like me to remind you to take out the garbage, but we've agreed that it's your job. I'll expect you to take it out before you leave for school."
JIMMY: How come I have to do it?
JANET: I know you don't like the job, but you are responsible for it, so I expect you to do it.
Janet's and Jimmy's feelings: satisfied.

8:00. Janet and Harry discuss the checking account error.

9:00. Jimmy has gone to school, and Janet plans her day. Karen, the next-door neighbor who borrows everything, calls. Her vacuum cleaner is broken and she needs to borrow Janet's.
JANET: I realize you're in a bind, but I'm tired of loaning out my household appliances. I'm afraid I can't loan it to you.
KAREN: But you used to give me what I needed.
JANET: Yes, I know I did, but I've decided to stop loaning out my things.
Janet's feelings: successful, able to stand up for herself and complete her daily tasks.

10:30. Janet goes to pick up Harry's shirts. She gives the laundry attendant a ten-dollar bill, and he hurriedly gives her change for a five.
JANET: I know you're busy, but you gave me change for a five when I gave you a ten.

ATTENDANT: No ma'am, you're wrong. I always check the bills before I make change.

JANET: I'm sure you want to be accurate in your work, but I know that I gave you a ten-dollar bill. If you're not willing to give me the proper change, I'd like to see the manager.

ATTENDANT: Well, he's busy.

JANET: I'll wait.

ATTENDANT: It may be a long time.

JANET: That's all right. I'll wait.

ATTENDANT: Why don't I just go ahead and give you the change?

JANET: That's fine with me.

Janet's feeling: in control of herself, successful.

12:00. Nancy, a community leader, calls to tell Janet that she is going to head up the neighborhood charity drive.

JANET: Nancy, I know you need volunteers and I'm sure I could do the job, but I'm not going to have the time, since I'm enrolling in college.

NANCY: Why would you do that? You've already been to college! What would your husband say?

JANET: I know you'd like to have me do it, but I don't have time for charity drives this year. You'll have to find someone else.

NANCY: I thought at least I could count on you.

JANET: I know you're disappointed, but I'm taking my education seriously now, so I won't have the time I used to for other jobs.

Janet's feeling: pleased for being so straight.

A Case Study in Assertiveness 97

2:30. Janet sits down to watch her favorite TV program. Karen comes in.

KAREN: Am I bothering you?

JANET: Yes. I'll have to talk with you later.

KAREN: Well, it won't take a minute.

JANET: I can see you want to chat, but I'm interested in this program and I don't want to talk right now.

Karen chatters on.

JANET: I don't believe you heard me. I'll call you and we can talk later.

Karen leaves.

Janet's feeling: pleased.

3:30. Jimmy rushes home from school demanding a ride to football practice.

JANET: Jimmy, I know you need to get to practice, but since I had no warning I won't be able to drive you today. You'll have to ride your bike.

JIMMY: But I'll be late.

JANET: I know you don't like to be late, but in the future you will have to give me advance notice.

4:00. Janet and Harry negotiate cocktails at home and eating out.

Janet's feeling: satisfied.

8:30. Janet and Harry negotiate fixing the fuse.

Janet's feeling: satisfied.

9:00. Janet tells Harry she wants to go back to school to take a course.

Janet's feeling: scared.

HARRY: I know you've been wanting to do that, but I'm worried about a drastic change in our life style. I wish you would wait another quarter.

JANET: Harry, I can see how you'd be concerned, but I've worked out a schedule that will force only a few adjustments on all of us, so I'd like to go ahead and register for one course.

HARRY: Well, if I won't lose all my favorite time with you, I guess it would be all right.

Janet's feelings: a little scared, but confident of her success.

11
Nonverbal Components of Assertiveness

Thus far only the verbal aspects of assertiveness have been emphasized—the words that are used to make an assertive response. It is equally important, however, to consider the nonverbal behaviors that accompany the statement. What you say verbally and what you say nonverbally must match if you are to make an effective, totally assertive statement.

Consider an employee asserting himself to his supervisor as he requests an increase in pay. His statement might be, "I realize that you have to make the final decisions in departmental raises, but I feel that I've done more than my share of the workload and that I'm entitled to a significantly higher raise than you outlined." Though this is an effective assertive statement, it would lose its strength if coupled with nonassertive nonverbal behavior. Typical nonassertive behavior would be for the employee to look out the window behind the supervisor or to look at the floor and speak in muted tones. Though the supervisor may be able to hear what the employee is saying, he will very likely read the nonverbal behavior and conclude that the employee does not mean what he said or does not need to be taken seriously.

The purpose of this chapter is to identify various nonverbal behaviors which when combined with verbal skills provide a complete assertive statement. Actions and words must go together. When the verbal and nonverbal aspects of being assertive are congruent, the statement is believable and there is no room for doubt. An individual who smiles while he tells you that he is angry presents an incongruent picture. He says one thing with his words and another with his behavior. He leaves it to you to decide whether to believe the smile or the angry words.

Another example might be the following: A friend spots you in a store and corners you. She tells you that you have been selected to serve as the director of the local Community Chest for your area. This is not a position that you want to accept, but she is very persistent and you feel pressured to respond to her. By now, you have learned how to make the assertive verbal response. It is important to pair it with appropriate nonverbal behavior so that there will be no misunderstanding when you refuse.

Here are some possible responses to the example:

Nonassertive Response

VERBAL	NONVERBAL
"I'm really not very good at talking to people, but if you can't find anyone else..."	Look away or down at floor; turn sideways; speak softly to avoid being heard; fidget.

Aggressive Response (Indirect)

"Well, I'm really very busy and I've done that job before. How about Marge? You know, she's new in town and it would be a terrific way for her to meet people."	Avoid eye contact; pretend to recognize someone across the store and rapidly excuse yourself; move away as you speak.

Aggressive Response (Direct)

"Who do you think you are? I'm surprised that you would even consider me for that. I won't do it!"	Stare at her while you talk; put your hands on your hips or point your finger at her while you answer; move directly toward her.

Assertive Response

"I can see that you're very eager to get a director, but I'm not interested in heading up the charity. I won't be able to accept the position, but I'll be happy to work for a couple of hours during the drive."	*Look her straight in the eye; face her squarely; give your response firmly and distinctly; stand still and be relaxed.*

A Verbal Response Model of Assertiveness

In the example you had four possible ways to respond to your friend: you could be nonassertive, directly aggressive, indirectly aggressive, or assertive. In each situation the verbal response and the nonverbal cues that would match that type of response were described. In the nonassertive response you might have looked away, trying to hedge or avoid responding, hoping that your friend might withdraw her request. Then you wouldn't have to say no; you could rely on the old mind-reading game. If you responded quietly enough perhaps she wouldn't hear. The nonverbal behavior accompanying the indirect aggressive response was designed to draw attention away from yourself to someone else. By moving away and at the same time suggesting that Marge should be the chairman, you can hope to slide out of the request without her even knowing what happened. In the direct aggressive response the nonverbal behavior conveyed a superior attitude, as you confronted her physically as well as verbally. Moving very quickly and pointing a finger at her while answering in a very loud voice so that others might hear would be an attempt to embarrass your friend. (Teachers and mothers often do this with children.) Again, you hope that she may withdraw her request or at least not bother you with it again.

In the assertive response you make direct eye contact the entire time you are verbalizing the statement. You speak firmly, standing comfortably on both feet and keeping about an arm's length between you. Speak very precisely. Your message will be communicated verbally and nonverbally. You do not have to give up your position or attack or retreat in any way.

In order to help you become aware of nonverbal behavior, try practicing some responses in front of a mirror. Imagine that you are responding to someone. Ask yourself whether you look convincing. Observe your eye contact and your stance and listen to your speech. Do you speak firmly at a moderate pace? Do you seem relaxed? Are you standing on both feet or are you shuffling around nervously?

Assertive nonverbal responses include the following:
1. Face the individual.
2. Make eye contact with him.
3. Take a few seconds before you speak to compose your answer.
4. Speak in a firm, pleasant tone of voice.
5. Present the statement clearly and moderately.
6. Match your facial cues with your verbal statement.

In short, "body language" is important and must be congruent with verbal language. Always be aware of how you look (eye contact), how you stand (body posture), and how you speak (voice quality).

12

Negotiation

The acquisition of skills in assertive behavior results in personal changes. One of the most challenging and difficult ways in which the ability to be assertive is tested is in ongoing relationships. It is relatively easy to learn to be assertive with the manager of a department store, the waiter in a restaurant, or the service manager of a car dealership. You may change your behavior in these situations without disturbing anyone's expectations of you. Being assertive in these kinds of situations is usually low in risk because they can be one-time confrontations. You can usually go to a different store, a different restaurant, or a new car dealership if your assertiveness doesn't pay off.

The true test, however, lies in your ability to be assertive with friends, family, or loved ones (see Chapter 14 on intimacy). When your family or close friends see changes in you, they are sometimes puzzled, angry, or frightened. Your family and friends expect predictability, and any change in you, however desirable, may cause confusion.

Any interaction between two or more people in which there is an ongoing relationship can become static. The participants in that relationship come to expect certain behaviors and attitudes from the other person or persons. For example, if a mother has learned to complain to her children before they provide help with household chores, that pattern of interaction will continue. Or if a close friend has learned through experience that he can borrow your golf clubs and not return them until you ask for them, this pattern will continue because of the history of the relationship of borrowing and not returning. In order to minimize the risk of confrontation or rejection from family and friends, it is vital that you tell them how you are going to be different (assertive) and how you would like them to respond to you. You do this by telling them what you have learned about assertiveness and how you have felt about the relationship in the past. A person who has learned to be assertive usually desires to continue his relationships, but in a different manner. He helps teach others how he wants the relationship to be different.

In order to minimize the risk of confrontation or rejection from family and friends it is vital that you tell them how you are going to be different and how they can change too. You do this by teaching them the assertive skills you have learned. A person who has learned to be assertive usually desires to continue his relationships but in a different manner. He therefore helps teach others how he wants them to be different.

Here are some examples:
1. You have a friend who continually imposes upon you by asking favors, yet never volunteers to help you when you are in need.
2. Your employer, a man whom you like and trust, continually asks you to take on additional work that requires your staying late or working weekends.
3. Your spouse always makes the decisions about where the two of you will take vacations.

Typically, people know only a limited number of ways of resolving their differences. These styles of resolving problems may not be evident in single interactions, but they are readily discernible in ongoing relationships such as those between a boss and secretary, a brother and sister, or a husband and wife. Conflicts between two individuals may begin with a new or unique disagreement, but after the second or third interaction between the parties, the conflict settles down to a repetitive and highly predictable style. Whether people think about it or not they rely on old, well-used styles of conflict resolution with which they have been more or less successful in the past.

Based on the nonassertive and aggressive styles of interacting identified in earlier chapters, the following are some of the ways these individuals resolve interpersonal conflicts:

1. Direct attack. This technique involves frightening the other person into submission with hostile and abusive language and/or gestures.

These attacks are marked by punitive statements that seek to scare him into withdrawing. For example: "How could you be so stupid as to have done that?" "You are the most selfish person I have ever met."

2. *Guilt induction.* A person using this technique seeks to cause the other person to feel guilty for what he has done or not done. Such interactions are marked by statements like these: "How could you have done that to me?" "You should have known better," or "If you loved me, you'd ..."

3. *Pouting.* Pouting—the old "silent treatment"—is employed by one of the parties in the conflict who acts hurt or who merely punishes the other by nonparticipation.

4. *Demand for mind-reading.* This is a subtle, indirect method whereby a participant indicates his desires in a very roundabout fashion in hopes that the other person will guess what's wrong and act accordingly. This style is often marked by asking questions rather than making clear statements.

5. *Playing martyr.* Playing martyr is indirectly trying to make the other person feel guilty for his request or his rejection of your request. Statements sound straightforward but the intent is to induce guilt. "Sure, take the car. Your mother and I just won't go out tonight." (Meaning: We wanted to use the car, so if you take it you'll have to pay the price of feeling guilty.) "It doesn't matter to me; you do what you think is right." (Meaning: It *does* matter to me, but do it your way.)

These are just a few of the more obvious techniques used to resolve interpersonal conflicts. All of these techniques have in common the individual's desire to solve the problem by withdrawing from the conflict, thus giving up or giving in.

The alternative technique in any of the aforementioned situations is negotiation. Negotiation is a process whereby the participants respect each other's rights in an honest, open interaction by sharing their thoughts and feelings concerning their differences. Negotiations are entered into in the belief that the interaction will benefit the relationship and the individuals involved. Each party is aware of his own goals and limits, but because of the ongoing relationship, compromises are essential.

The following is an example of what happens when two assertive people find themselves in disagreement. Here is a potentially explosive situation between husband and wife, Harry and Janet. Janet, having learned that she could succeed in school, now desires to attend the university on a full-time basis to obtain a degree. Harry, however, is set on having a third child and leaving the situation status quo, with him as the major breadwinner and her as housewife and mother. The following excerpt from their conversation shows the process by which they negotiate their disagreement. Each is aware of his own goals and limits as they make their compromises.

JANET (*anxious*): Harry, I know you've got a busy week, but I want time to talk with you. When would be a good time?

HARRY: Now is fine with me.

JANET (*scared*): I realize that what I'm going to say may come as a surprise to you, but I've done so well in my course this quarter that I want to continue on a full-time basis and get my degree.

HARRY (*surprised*): Yes, I am surprised. I can see you're excited, but this seems like a sudden change in plans. I'd like some more information.

JANET (*excited*): Well, I really like being back in school, and I've been encouraged by my professor to pursue my degree.

HARRY (*concerned*): I can see how it would be fun for you to be back in school, but I don't see how you'll manage the house, the kids, and your schoolwork too. I think you'd better reconsider your decision for now anyhow.

JANET (*angry*): I knew you'd have some reservations, but I resent your assumption that I'm responsible for the entire management of the house and the children. I would need you to take more responsibility for both the children and the house.

HARRY (*defiant*): I can see that you'd need help, but I don't want household responsibilities now with all I have on my mind at work. I'd rather drop the subject entirely.

JANET (*hurt*): Well, I'm hurt that you want to drop a subject that is obviously of vital importance to me. I want to do something special with my life, and getting my degree will help me to do that. I don't want to be only a mother and a wife. I also want a career.

HARRY (*disappointed*): This degree is sounding really important to you, but I thought we were planning to have another child soon. When we got married our plans were to settle down, buy a house, and have three children. Now all of a sudden you've changed your mind! I'm disappointed.

JANET (*fearful*): Yes, I know you're hurt and angry because I changed my mind. I've considered my decision for a long time, but I didn't talk to you because I was afraid you'd feel this way. I don't want to spend five years rearing another child and delaying going back to school.

HARRY (*defensive*): Finishing your degree seems to be more important to you than your family.

JANET (*concerned*): Harry, you know you and the children are very important to me, but having another child is a lower priority in my life now than getting my degree and beginning a career.

HARRY (*relieved*): Well, I feel better to hear that having another child is a lower priority rather than not even being an option for you. I'd like to discuss the baby at a later time.

JANET (*clear*): I know how important that child is to you, and I'm willing to talk about it later when I'm finishing my degree.

HARRY (*scared*): There you go again. You sure are set on that degree. I just don't understand what's happened to you.

JANET (*uncertain*): I know the changes in me scare you, but I want to get my degree to contribute to my family in a way different from what I am now. I'm not sure exactly how that will be, but I know that it begins with my going to school.

HARRY (*insecure*): Does that mean you won't need us anymore? That you'll become one of those self-sufficient, independent women?

JANET (*scared and excited*): Well, I probably will become more independent but that doesn't mean I won't still need and love my family. I'm scared of changes, too, but I'm also excited to be trying something new. I know you've already said you're unwilling to shift any household responsibilities to yourself, but I would like a commitment on your part to help more with the children.

HARRY (*clear*): Well, if you return to school I'm willing to spend some weekends with the children, but I'm not going to baby-sit with them during the week.

JANET (*aware*): I appreciate the pressure you feel you're under, but I'm not going to be able to watch the children during the week so I'd like to hire a part-time housekeeper to baby-sit and do the housework.

HARRY (*angry*): That's all well and good, but where's all this money coming from?

JANET (*clear and supportive*): I knew that would be an important concern, so I refigured our budget to include the additional expenses for a housekeeper and for my tuition. It will simply mean putting less in savings for the next two years.

HARRY (*struggling for control*): I'm not sure that's a good idea. What if something unexpected happened and we needed the money?

JANET (*prepared*): I know that a large savings account is important to you, but I feel if we need the money I'll get a part-time job.

HARRY (*uncertain but supportive*): You certainly have worked things out. I'm beginning to see how important this degree is to you, and there's no way to change your mind. I don't like it, and I feel uncertain about our future together, but if you'll continue to talk with me about how I feel, then I want you to know I'll support you the best way I can.

The preceding example shows the process of negotiation between Harry and Janet, who have a clear disagreement about a basic aspect of their relationship but who are willing to negotiate a compromise. Effective negotiation requires that certain guidelines be followed. First, it is helpful for one party to request discussion time of an appropriate duration. Janet requested time to talk with Harry and he accepted.

Second, Janet took responsibility for making an assertive statement in presenting her request. This request was her desire to attend school on a full-time basis to get her degree. She asked clearly for what she wanted.

The next step in negotiating was Harry's reflection of what he heard Janet saying, especially how she felt. He then offered his own feelings and suggested an alternative proposal (to reconsider the decision for now).

Janet's next step could have been to accept his suggestion, offer a counterproposal, or return to the original request. She was unwilling to reconsider, so she returned to her original proposal and outlined some of the changes it would necessitate.

A negotiation continues back and forth until an acceptable compromise is reached. Both parties need not agree on the outcome, but they have mutual respect and trust that the compromise is the best possible solution presently available. The greatest deterrent to negotiation is getting scared, changing the subject and ending up in irrelevancy.

Old problems, accusations, and blaming all are irrelevant in negotiations and detract from clear, straightforward communication.

These guidelines apply to any encounter between two assertive people. First is a request for time by the initiator and agreement by the other. Second is a clear statement by the initiator of what he wants. Third is an answer of acceptance or a counterproposal by the other person. Fourth is acceptance, counterproposal, or return to the original proposal by the initiator. Steps 2, 3, and 4 continue until a compromise satisfactory to both parties is reached. Such a compromise may even be to stop negotiation and continue it later, or to realize that there is no mutually acceptable alternative to the present problem.

13

Self-Diagnosis

Through the illustrations in earlier chapters we have presented an assertive means of responding that we called the verbal response model. The verbal response model was based on the individual's desire to be assertive, to change his behavior from nonassertive or aggressive to a mode that protected his rights as well as the rights of others.

The purpose of this chapter is to help you personalize the verbal response model. Here you have an opportunity to identify specific situations that you wish to change by being more assertive.

Part 1 outlined your three basic rights. All of the situations in your life involving assertiveness are based on these rights. If you change your attitudes toward others by acting on these rights and at the same time use the model presented in this book, you can change your behavior.

Remember that you have the following personal rights:
1. *The right to rectify a wrong or injustice.* By incorporating this attitude into your values you will be able to stand up for yourself.
2. *The right to refuse.* This basic right allows you to set your own limits, to say no when it is in your best interests.
3. *The right to request.* This right enables you to set personal goals and ask for what you want.

As you consider these three rights, think about how they can change your relationships with others. Are you a spouse, a customer, an employer? Are you a friend to one person, a parent to another, a teacher to another? As you think of your roles in relation to others, consider specific situations that have occurred between you and other people. For instance, do you cringe at the thought of refusing a dinner invitation from your parents? Do you avoid returning items to a store? Do you feel manipulated by your spouse when you make a request? If these or other such situations leave you feeling uncomfortable, dissatisfied, or unhappy, then you are probably failing to exercise one or more of your basic rights.

On the next page is a matrix that can be used to help you identify specific areas in which you wish to be more assertive. Select a person from the column on the left and a personal right from the row across the top. Locate the square where the two intersect. Briefly describe the situation that you wish to change. Name the person involved and describe the interaction between the two of you and how you feel in that situation.

For example, if you have difficulty saying no to a friend who continually abuses your right of privacy by uninvited visits to your apartment, you would write the following in the box at the intersection of *Friend* and *Refusal*: "Bill invites himself over; I do nothing to stop him. Feelings: helpless, angry."

Then write a three-part assertive response to the situation that would enable you to stand up for yourself and change the situation.

SELF-DIAGNOSIS OF ASSERTIVE PROBLEMS

	RECTIFICATION	REFUSAL	REQUEST
Employee			
Supervisor			
Spouse			
Salesperson			
Child			
Friend			
Acquaintance			
Other			

Write a three-part response to each situation on the matrix that you wish to change. Obviously, the last and final step in being assertive is to apply these responses, with appropriate nonverbal behavior, in an actual encounter.

14

Assertiveness: An Avenue to Intimacy

Intimacy—in a book on assertiveness? Yes! How often we have heard individuals say that they can be assertive with everyone except the people they are closest to—mother, father, spouse, children. Most individuals are able to learn to be assertive with people with whom they have minimal contact. The idea of asserting rights in close relationships is automatically rejected for a multitude of reasons:

"I can't hurt her feelings."

"He wouldn't understand."

"I never put myself first when it comes to my children."

"My mother would become ill if I didn't call her twice a day."

"If they were my parents I'd tell them not to stay, but since they're my husband's parents I can't."

"I've never stood up to my mother—she'd be so hurt!"

"My children expect me to baby-sit with their children every weekend. I can't disappoint them."

The purpose of this book is to teach you to be assertive and to protect your rights not only with salesmen, supervisors, and acquaintances, but in *all* relationships. Failure to honor your rights in close relationships demands that others read your mind or that they take care of you in some way to protect you. If you don't take care of yourself and expect others to do so, you are left feeling disappointed, frustrated, and hurt when someone you love fails to figure out what you wanted. One of the ways in which you may inappropriately protect yourself is by becoming distant in a close relationship and not asking for what you want.

Mary, a forty-year-old married woman, dreaded visits from her mother. Her mother would arrive unexpectedly and stay for indefinite periods of time, ignoring all Mary's subtle cues to get her to leave. Each visit was filled with anxiety and anger for Mary while her mother seemed oblivious to her daughter's distress. When we asked Mary in a counseling session about her own rights, she said, "I couldn't refuse to let her come. She has nowhere else to go." Mary's response was an extreme one. We worked with Mary to identify her own goals in the visits with her mother. It turned out that her goal was to have her mother visit on a prearranged date for a specific length of time agreeable to both of them. She did have a right to request a specified visit from her mother. Mary then asked her mother to comply, and her mother responded with surprise but agreed. The following visit was the first pleasant one for Mary. She had decided her own limits, set her goal, and talked with her mother. Thus, she did not have to distance herself through anger, hurt, or frustration.

Being assertive in a relationship lays the foundation for intimacy. Because Mary previously had been unwilling to be assertive with her mother (for fear of losing what she believed was a close relationship) she risked being distant because of the barriers she put in the way and actually impeded the relationship by her anger and anxiety. The fallacy inherent in nonassertive behavior is the belief that you will therefore not hurt the other person and that he will therefore like you and be close to you. In reality, however, unless the other person knows how you feel, what you want, and what your limits are, he knows only the fantasy you project instead of the person you really are. That does not form the basis for a close relationship.

As you build close relationships (they don't automatically unfold) there is a critical demand that you say where you are and what you want. When a couple decide on a vacation, they must both express their feelings and preferences if they are to reach a mutual decision. If the husband assumes that his wife knows where he wants to go and why, he distances himself from her.

Intimacy is based on nonpossessive caring for another with trust in both of you as people. Being assertive with one another leads you toward—not away from—one another. Because you both continue to hear and be heard, to say where you are and what you want in the relationship, there is a greater opportunity for closeness than there is when you must guess what the other wants.

In casual relationships you may find that you set firm limits on what you will and won't do but often in close relationships your willingness to negotiate your limits is crucial to strengthening the relationship.

Being assertive does not involve conning or manipulating, but rather genuinely sharing who you are and what your goals and limits are. Because of your awareness of who you are and what you want to have happen, you are able to maintain control within yourself. Therefore you don't need to manipulate the other person. You will not always attain your goal, but the value and the mutual caring in the relationship make negotiation possible. Both of you can move closer to each other without jeopardizing yourselves or the relationship.

Index

Action, 69, 83-89
Aggressive, 28, 38, 48-56, 87-88
Anger, 7
Appease, 40
Assertive, vii, 28, 31, 46, 58-65, 88, 89, 99, 102, 104, 106, 114
Assertive response, 71, 77, 85

Conflict, 69, 77-82, 85, 106
Communication, 11, 22, 64
Confrontation, 20, 40, 105

Empathy, 68, 69, 71-76, 85

Fear: of embarassment, 31-32; of expectation, 21; of rejection, vii, 2, 11, 23, 39, 42, 105

Guilt, 7, 39, 41, 45, 52, 107

Individual rights, vii, 3
Intimacy, 118-121

Intimidator, 48, 49, 50, 55, 56

Manipulator, 38, 51-53, 56, 121
Model, 68, 114

Negotiation, 104-113
Nonassertive, vii, 11, 14, 28, 31, 39-46, 58, 88, 89, 101, 106
Nonverbal, 99-103

Passivity, 38
Personal rights, 15, 59, 115
Placate, 40

Rectify, 15-18, 24, 58, 61
Refusal, 15, 18-20, 24, 45, 58, 60
Rejection, vii, 2, 7, 10, 20
Request, 15, 20-23, 24, 58, 102
Responsibility, 9, 62, 90
Rights, 10, 15,

Self-awareness, 59
Selfish, 7

123